Justice in Metastate Era: AI, Self-Litigation & Legal Ethics

Slava Solodkiy

Published by Slava Solodkiy, 2024.

While every precaution has been taken in the preparation of this book, the publisher assumes no responsibility for errors or omissions, or for damages resulting from the use of the information contained herein.

JUSTICE IN METASTATE ERA: AI, SELF-LITIGATION & LEGAL ETHICS

First edition. November 20, 2024.

Copyright © 2024 Slava Solodkiy.

ISBN: 979-8230541578

Written by Slava Solodkiy.

Table of Contents

Justice in Metastate Era: AI, Self-Litigation & Legal Ethics 1

1. An Online-Court in Singapore, or Justice-as-a-Service: A New Paradigm? 8

2. 'Lawyers Herculeses' and ' Hercules the Judge' 33

3. The Paradox of Self-Representation: Advancing Fairness in Legal Systems 51

7. Self-Litigant Costs Reimbursement 94

8. The Cynicism of It All: The Domino Effect of Impunity 95

9. Confidentiality Clauses and Other Fairy Tales: An Open Letter .. 96

10. Filed for Personal Bankruptcy & Gave Up: When 'Winning' Means Losing Everything..99

11. How Powerful Crooks Weaponize the Law to Silence Critics .. 101

12. My Personal Bankruptcy in the UK, US, and Singapore 113

13. The Predictability of R&T's Tactics: The Theater of Arival's Absurd.. 116

14. Another Day, Another Lawsuit Against Me – How Predictable! 125

15. A Lone Fighter Against the Legal Giants: The Ally in Your Corner for 20$ 131

16. The AI Advocate: Justice Reimagined - Self-Litigation, AI, and the Pursuit of Fairness.. 136

17. The Unexpected Harmony of Order: My Life as an Unlikely Self-Litigant 141

Epilogue: 'The Shadow of Justice' 148

Rethinking Justice in Metastate Era: AI, Self-Litigation & Legal Ethics

Unrepresented But Unbowed: **A Self-Litigant's Guide to AI**, SLAPP & New Fairness

by **Slava Solodkiy**

ChatGPT Goes to Court-as-a-Service: Tales of a Self-Litigant [Selected Chapters] Read the full story here[1]:

---

1. https://l.nansen.id/bookEng

Dedicated to the most professional and exemplary lawyers in Singapore—champions of justice, guardians of legal ethics, and true embodiments of the spirit of the law. These 'Lawyer-Hercules' stand tall, 'just doing their job,' serving as pillars of Singaporean society and role models for the next generation of legal minds.

Tao Tao <tao.tao@rajahtann.com>, Ashwin Kumar Menon <ashwin.menon@rajahtann.com>, Andre Yeap <andre.yeap@rajahtann.com>, Jansen Chow <jansen.chow@rajahtann.com>, Jason Lim <jason.lim@rajahtann.com>, Ong Sheng Bo <shengbo.ong@rajahtann.com>, Su Ann Chua <su.ann@characterist.com>, Dominic Chan <dominic@characterist.com>

Form and Formality Pte Ltd

Perhaps a modern legal scholar should write a dissertation titled "*The Specter of Formalism Haunting Jurisprudence: A Neo-Marxist-Nietzschean Critique of R&T Lawyering.*" It would certainly be a conversation starter!

'*Form certainly determines content*' - but even Marx, Engels, Hegel, Nietzsche, and Kant would be surprised (shocked and turning in their graves and crying bloody tears!) at how this phrase is understood and has been interpreted in the understanding of law (the prevalence of details, processes, and procedures over content and essence - the frantic prevalence of the letter of the law over the spirit of the law!) by lawyers of Arival Pte Ltd from Rajah & Tann and Characterist.

They say "*The map is not the territory,*" (I like '*there is no land before arrival*' more) a concept famously explored by Alfred Korzybski. But even Korzybski, along with philosophers like Wittgenstein and Derrida, would be astonished at how this idea has been twisted by legal bureaucrats at R&T representing Arival Pte Ltd — where the paperwork has become more important than the actual work! They're probably turning in their graves, aghast at the elevation of form over substance.

Why did the Hegelian cross the road? To get to the aufgehoben other side! But seriously, it's a tragicomic irony that the very thinkers who emphasized dialectical reasoning and the interplay of form and content are now invoked to justify a rigid, formalistic approach to law. One can imagine Marx chuckling at the "alienation" of law from its intended purpose, while Nietzsche might see it as a manifestation of the "will to power" of bureaucratic procedures.

'Form determines content'

'Form determines content': The concept was extensively discussed in the works of Karl Marx and Friedrich Engels.

For **Hegel**, the concept of form and content play a key role and are inextricably linked: content is constantly evolving and taking on new form, and form in turn can determine how content manifests itself. In The Science of Logic, Hegel wrote that "form is not something external to content", emphasizing their unity.

Kant considered the concepts of form and content within the framework of the theory of cognition. For him, form was a category structuring sensory data, and content was the data of experience itself. In the Critique of Pure Reason, Kant explains that the form of knowledge is given by the a priori structures of reason, while the content comes from sense experience. Thus, form determines how we perceive content.

With **Nietzsche**, the idea of form and content is evident in his thoughts on language, art and culture. He argued that form can conceal content or even determine how content is perceived. In The Birth of Tragedy and other works, Nietzsche discusses how the form of art affects the expression of human experience.

With admiration and gratitude to the lawyers of Singapore, whose commitment to justice and the spirit of the law makes a real difference.

[Selected Chapters] Read the full story here[2]: https://l.Nansen.id/bookEng[3]

Listen me on Spotify: https://l.Nansen.id/spotify[4]

---

2. https://l.nansen.id/bookEng

3. https://l.nansen.id/bookEng

4. https://l.nansen.id/spotify

Part 1: Judge Hercules Meets AI: the Future of Law in the Age of Self-Litigation

It started with a quartet, then a quintet, now a magnificent seven[5][[1]]: Tao Tao[6], Ashwin Menon[7], Jansen Chow[8], Dominic Chan[9], and other esteemed lawyers from Rajah & Tann Asia[10] and Characterist LLC[11] - a lone firm multiplied into two. All against little ol' me. To sue or not to sue? The question I keep posing to them, and the esteemed The Law Society of Singapore[12] (no answer yet, hm) echoes unanswered: where lies the elusive boundary between the rigid letter of the law and its noble spirit? Rules, details, procedures - sacred, no doubt. But shouldn't substance prevail over form? Where is the lawyer who, akin to a doctor bound by the Hippocratic Oath, champions the underdog, upholding the presumption of innocence? And where is the lawyer who, with a discerning eye, witnesses justice being perverted into a tool of extortion and yet, turns a blind eye? The Nuremberg trials established it long ago - "I was just following orders" is no refuge. The Wirecard scandal underscored it with indelible ink - money has a stench, and a pungent one at that! But alas, my esteemed friends at Rajah & Tann (and Characterist now too) seem blissfully unaware of the odor clinging to their fees, the spirit of the law trampled underfoot, and the ethical compass spinning wildly off its axis.

---

5. https://www.linkedin.com/posts/vsolodkiy_a-lone-fighter-against-the-legal-giants-activity-7244399907791339522-jzee/

6. https://www.linkedin.com/in/taotao52/

7. https://www.linkedin.com/in/ashwin-menon-94b1221a3/

8. https://www.linkedin.com/in/jansen-chow-9643a9139/

9. https://www.linkedin.com/in/darrendominicchan/

10. https://www.linkedin.com/company/rajah-&-tann/

11. https://www.linkedin.com/in/characterist-llc/

12. https://www.linkedin.com/company/the-law-society-of-singapore/

An injured hiker limps into view. "I was bitten by a snake!"
The paramedic nods. "Do you have the snake's identification for our records?"
"It slithered away!!!"
"Without proper identification, administering antivenom violates our protocol."

1. An Online-Court in Singapore, or Justice-as-a-Service: A New Paradigm?

Whenever people talk about network states, or better, metastates, or chartered cities, Estonia is often mentioned[1], but I more often use Singapore as an example[2]. If you separate politics (discussions about values and strategies) from functions (specific services) within a state, you can perfect each "toothbrush" (to use Silicon Valley parlance) and make it scalable far beyond a single state.

Too often, there's too much debate – does the service simply work or not, is it expensive or cheap, fast or slow? Debates about the eternal are certainly important, but both sides will only benefit if politics are uprooted and separated from the services provided by the state (security, elections, healthcare, education, monetary and fiscal policy, etc).

I have many wonderful stories about the efficiency of various Singaporean government services - like the IRS tax authority, the MAS financial regulator, health support through nutrition, and quality of life through domestic helpers... I could list examples for a very long time - and often raise the question that Singapore does some things so well that: why shouldn't it become more and more government-as-a-service? Scale and export individual services to other countries - such as the SingPass digital identity project, or Justice-as-a-Service[3][2]?

---

1. https://www.linkedin.com/pulse/ukraines-next-big-export-fedorovs-diia-pioneers-vladislav-solodkiy-nxuae/?trackingId=6cIBcT07R1OkqrkKqCxtuw%3D%3D

2. https://www.techinasia.com/talk/lifesreda-emigrussia-inspirasia

3. https://www.linkedin.com/pulse/online-court-singapore-justice-as-a-service-new-vladislav-solodkiy-my6je/

I recently filed a number of lawsuits in SG Courts[4] - State (Magistrate and District) Courts, and High Court (HC/OC 618/2024). Once again, I was surprised at how, when faced with another government service in Singapore, you feel like a client! Yes, a client - you can directly see how important it is for the state not only for you to have access to justice, but also for it to be clear and convenient for you.

Just imagine - claims can be filed independently (without expensive lawyers - everything is quite clear and logical), and online (both document flow and hearings are often remote!). I write emails to the court myself with questions or explanations - and the court representatives politely and quickly (often within 2-3 days!) respond, in accessible language, and delving into what you wrote.

When you first file lawsuits, the CrimsonLogic Pte Ltd[5] employees who help those who have chosen the self-litigation route in the State Courts of Singapore[6] or Supreme Court not only help you figure out how and what to file, but also, in my case, personally provide moral support. Really! People see that you are not a lawyer, you are nervous, you don't always know and understand everything - and then I hear: "Hey, what are you doing, relax, you're already here, you came, you prepared well, now we will help you fill everything out correctly. Don't worry, no one will chase you away from here until we help you." Can you imagine that? I don't know how it is in your country - but I've lived in several countries, and everywhere this would simply be a miracle or a fairy tale, no one would believe it!

Like in a good mobile app - I not only receive all sorts of auto-reminders, but also all sorts of nice thank-yous, for example,

---

4. https://www.linkedin.com/company/sgcourts/

5. https://www.linkedin.com/company/crimsonlogic/

6. https://www.linkedin.com/company/state-courts-of-singapore/

"thank you for preparing well for self-submission, we appreciate that you care about our work too."

I have seen several times when people with disabilities approached - and they were immediately accepted not only without a queue, but also a special person came to them, listened, understood, helped formulate thoughts and the problem.

It is clear that a good attitude should not be confused with an already won your case - but no matter how my lawsuits in Singapore end, whether I win or lose, I am already very grateful to everyone who constantly helps me offline and online to protect my rights: CrimsonLogic dreamteam, registrars and other employees of the State Courts and the Supreme Court. Any legal process is such a stress, but here specific people, with the help of new technologies, are constantly thinking (not only about the process of legal proceedings and justice itself, but also) about you personally: so that it is clear, convenient, and cheap (yes, yes, very affordable for everyone!) for you.

And most importantly - on the merits! I feel it every time - that they hear me. Yes, sometimes they agree, sometimes they don't: but definitely any of my requests did not go unnoticed or rejected simply on a formal basis.

The use of AI and ML algorithms in judicial decisions presents both opportunities and challenges. While they have the potential to enhance fairness and efficiency, significant concerns about transparency, bias, and ethics must be addressed. Moving forward, it will be crucial to strike a balance between leveraging the strengths of machine learning and maintaining the essential human elements of justice and accountability. Robust oversight, ethical considerations, and legal safeguards will be key to ensuring that algorithms are used in a way that enhances rather than undermines the principles of justice.

Purpose of Self-Litigation in Singapore

The creation of the self-litigation or litigation-in-person option in Singapore (and in several other jurisdictions) is not specifically designed as a tool to "defend" ordinary people from wealthier opponents with more resources, such as large companies or individuals who can afford expensive lawyers, however, it does play a role in leveling the playing field to some extent by ensuring that everyone has access to justice, regardless of their financial means.

Government Support for Self-Represented Litigants in Singapore (Against Powerful Opponents)

The government, through the Community Justice Centre (CJC) and other initiatives, provides resources to help self-represented litigants navigate the legal process. This includes access to pro bono legal advice, simplified forms, and online guides.

1. **Access to Justice:** This right is fundamental to the legal system and is intended to prevent justice from being available only to those who can afford legal representation.
2. **Cost Savings:** Self-representation can help individuals save on legal fees, which can be prohibitively expensive, especially in complex cases. This is particularly important in situations where the potential cost of hiring a lawyer might deter someone from pursuing a legitimate legal claim.

While self-litigation is designed to provide access to the courts, it does trying to protect against the challenges posed when facing a well-resourced opponent, such as a large company or a wealthy individual:

1. **Resource Disparity:** Wealthier opponents can often afford

to hire experienced legal teams, engage in extensive legal research, and pursue strategies that can be time-consuming and costly for a self-represented litigant to counter (self-represented litigant may struggle to navigate the procedures, legal arguments, and evidentiary requirements needed to effectively argue their case).
2. **Potential for Strategic Use of Resources:** There is a risk that wealthier parties might use their resources to exhaust the self-represented litigant, for example, by filing numerous motions, engaging in extensive discovery, or dragging out the legal process, which could lead the self-represented litigant to give up due to time and financial constraints.

While self-representation is an option, Singapore also provides legal aid and various forms of assistance for those who qualify. This can include free or subsidized legal representation, access to legal clinics, and resources provided by the Community Justice Centre (CJC). To address some of these challenges, the Singaporean government and judiciary have implemented several measures regarding self-litigation route:

1. **Simplified Procedures:** In certain types of cases, such as small claims or certain matters, procedures have been simplified to make it easier for self-represented litigants to manage their cases.
2. **Judicial Discretion:** Judges in Singaporean courts are aware of the challenges faced by self-represented litigants and quite often may exercise discretion to ensure that cases are handled fairly, although they must remain impartial and cannot provide legal advice.

While the option for self-litigation in Singapore is not specifically intended to protect individuals from powerful opponents, it does provide a crucial means of access to justice for those who cannot afford expensive legal representation. However, the challenges of self-representation, particularly when facing a well-resourced opponent, remain significant, and the inherent complexities and potential for strategic resource use by wealthier parties can still pose difficulties for self-represented litigants.

History and Advantages of Self-Litigation in Terms of Civil Rights

Self-litigation, or litigation-in-person, has a significant history tied to civil rights and access to justice. This approach has played a key role in ensuring that individuals, regardless of their financial means or ability to secure legal representation, can still access the legal system and defend their rights.

1. **Historical Origins:** The right to self-representation has roots in the common law tradition, where courts recognized that every individual should have the opportunity to present their case, whether or not they could afford a lawyer. This principle was established to ensure fairness and prevent the legal system from being accessible only to those with resources.
2. **Civil Rights Movements:** During various civil rights movements, particularly in the 20th century, self-litigation became a vital tool for individuals, especially who were marginalized or disenfranchised. In many instances, individuals representing themselves were able to bring attention to issues of discrimination, injustice, and inequality, which might otherwise have been ignored if they were unable to secure legal representation.
3. **International Recognition:** The right to self-representation has been recognized in various international legal frameworks and human rights conventions, emphasizing its

importance as a fundamental aspect of access to justice.
4. **Empowerment of Individuals:** One of the primary achievements of self-litigation is that it provides access to justice for individuals who cannot afford an expensive lawyer. This ensures that economic barriers do not prevent people from seeking redress or defending themselves in court. Self-litigation empowers individuals by allowing them to take control of their legal matters. This can be particularly significant in civil rights cases, where the individual may feel that the legal system is biased or unresponsive to their needs. Representing oneself can be a powerful assertion of autonomy and rights.
5. **Highlighting Systemic Issues:** Cases where individuals have represented themselves have sometimes brought attention to broader systemic issues within the legal system or society. By navigating the system on their own, self-represented litigants may expose barriers, biases, or unfair practices that might not be as apparent when cases are handled by lawyers. There have been instances where self-represented litigants have succeeded in setting legal precedents or contributing to legal reforms. For example, landmark cases in various jurisdictions have been brought by individuals acting without lawyers, leading to significant changes in the law, particularly in areas of civil rights and liberties.
6. **Increased Legal Literacy:** The self-litigation process often leads to a better understanding of legal rights and the legal system among the general public. As more individuals engage directly with the law, there is a broader dissemination of legal knowledge, which can contribute to a more informed and engaged citizenry.

The history and achievements of self-litigation are deeply intertwined with the broader struggle for civil rights and access to justice. By allowing individuals to represent themselves, the legal system upholds a fundamental principle that justice should be accessible to all, not just to those who can afford legal representation. While self-litigation presents challenges, it remains a crucial aspect of ensuring fairness and equity in the legal system.

Encouragement of Simplified Procedures in Singapore

The prevalence of self-litigation has sometimes driven courts to simplify procedures and make legal processes more accessible. This can include the development of plain-language forms, the provision of legal aid resources, and the establishment of self-help centers, all of which contribute to a more accessible justice system.

In Singapore, while the courts provide certain accommodations and guidance to self-represented litigants (litigants-in-person), it's not entirely accurate to say that the government allows them to bypass all formal obligations, however, the courts do make efforts to ensure that the process is fair and that justice is not delayed unnecessarily by opponents with more resources. Here's a clearer understanding of how this works:

- **Flexibility for Self-Represented Litigants:** The Singapore courts understand that self-represented litigants may not have the same legal expertise as lawyers. As a result, the courts may offer some flexibility in procedural matters, particularly in lower courts like the State Courts or for less complex cases. Judges may provide guidance on procedural aspects and may be more lenient with procedural errors, as long as the core substance of the case is clear.

- **Focus on the Essence:** While self-represented litigants are still required to follow the rules of court, there is an emphasis on ensuring that the essence of the claim is not lost due to technicalities. Judges may help focus the proceedings on the key issues at hand rather than getting bogged down in procedural minutiae. However, this does not mean that all formal obligations can be ignored; fundamental rules, such as those related to evidence and legal argumentation, must still be followed.

- **Preventing Abuse of Process by Opposing Parties via Judicial Management of the Case:** Singaporean judges play an active role in managing cases to ensure that they are conducted efficiently and fairly. If a party with more resources tries to delay proceedings through excessive objections, re-applications, or other tactics, the judge has the discretion to intervene. This includes setting timelines for submissions, limiting the number of procedural motions, and ensuring that the case progresses without unnecessary delays.

- **Case Conferences and Pre-Trial Management:** In civil cases, especially in the High Court, judges often hold case conferences to streamline the issues, set deadlines, and address any procedural matters early in the process. This helps prevent one party from dragging out the proceedings unnecessarily.

- **Summary Judgment and Strike-Out Applications:** If a defense is deemed to be without merit, the court can grant a summary judgment or strike out the defense without going through a full trial. This mechanism prevents frivolous or vexatious actions from being used to delay justice.

- **Costs Implications:** The court may also impose costs orders on parties who engage in tactics designed to delay proceedings. This serves as a deterrent against using procedural tactics to wear down an opponent.

- **Simplified Trials for Certain Cases:** For certain types of cases, such as small claims, the process is deliberately simplified to make it more accessible for self-represented litigants. These simplified trials focus on the substance of the dispute without getting overly technical.

While the Singaporean legal system does provide some leniency and support to self-represented litigants, the courts do make efforts to ensure that the essence of a claim is not lost due to technicalities and that wealthier opponents cannot unduly delay proceedings. The overall aim is to ensure fairness, efficiency, and access to justice for all parties involved.

CrimsonLogic, through its eLitigation system and other technological services, plays a critical role in enabling and supporting self-litigation in Singapore. By providing an accessible, user-friendly platform for filing and managing legal cases, CrimsonLogic helps self-represented litigants navigate the complexities of the legal system more efficiently and effectively. This support is crucial in ensuring that individuals, regardless of their legal expertise or financial means, can pursue justice in the Singaporean courts.

Support for Self-Represented Litigants in Singapore

In Singapore, "self-litigation" or "litigation-in-person" refers to the legal process where an individual represents themselves in court without the assistance of an expensive lawyer. This can occur in both the State Courts and the High Court.

1. **No Legal Representation:** The litigant acts as their own lawyer, taking on all responsibilities typically handled by legal counsel, such as preparing legal documents, filing court papers, and arguing the case in court.
2. **Legal Rights:** Individuals have the right to represent themselves in all types of cases, whether civil or criminal, and in any level of court, including the State Courts and the High Court.
3. **Court's Role:** The courts may exercise a degree of leniency towards self-represented litigants in terms of procedural matters, but this is limited. Singapore provides some resources to help self-represented litigants, such as online guides, court forms, and legal clinics where individuals can receive free legal advice. The Community Justice Centre (CJC) is one such resource that offers support.

In the State Courts, self-litigation is more common, particularly in cases involving small claims, the procedures are generally more straightforward compared to the High Court. While self-litigation is allowed in the High Court, it is less common due to the complexity of the cases typically handled at this level, such as large civil claims, and appeals.

CrimsonLogic plays an essential role in supporting self-litigation in Singapore by providing the technological infrastructure and platforms that facilitate access to the legal system. Here's how CrimsonLogic contributes to self-litigation:

- **eLitigation System:** CrimsonLogic developed and manages the eLitigation system, which is an electronic filing and case management system used by the Singapore courts. This platform is crucial for self-represented litigants (litigants-in-person) because it allows them to file legal documents online, manage their cases, and access court records without needing to visit the court physically.

- **User-Friendly Interface:** The eLitigation platform is designed to be user-friendly, which helps self-represented litigants navigate the legal process more easily. The system provides step-by-step guidance on how to file documents, pay court fees, and comply with procedural requirements, which is particularly valuable for those without legal training.

- **Access to Information:** Through CrimsonLogic's platforms, self-represented litigants can access a wealth of legal information, including procedural guides, templates, and FAQs that help them understand how to prepare and present their cases.

- **Document Generation:** Some CrimsonLogic services offer automated document generation tools that assist litigants in creating the necessary legal documents by filling out forms with relevant details. This reduces the likelihood of procedural errors and helps ensure that the documents are in the correct format.

- **Legal Assistance Integration:** CrimsonLogic's platforms are often integrated with other legal support services, such as those provided by the Community Justice Centre (CJC) or Legal Aid Bureau. This integration allows self-represented litigants to access additional help if they need legal advice or assistance with complex issues.

- **Streamlining Processes:** By enabling online filings and case management, CrimsonLogic helps streamline the legal process, reducing the need for multiple court visits and minimizing delays. This is particularly beneficial for self-represented litigants, who might otherwise be overwhelmed by the procedural aspects of their cases.

- **Timely Notifications:** The eLitigation system also ensures that litigants receive timely notifications about court dates, deadlines, and other important developments in their cases, helping them stay on track and avoid missing critical steps.

- **Reduced Costs:** By providing an electronic platform for litigation, CrimsonLogic helps reduce the costs associated with self-representation, such as printing, courier fees, and time spent traveling to court. This makes the litigation process more accessible to individuals who might not have the financial resources to engage in traditional litigation.

- **Remote Access:** The ability to access court documents and manage cases remotely is particularly valuable for those who may have difficulty attending court in person due to work, health, or other constraints.

Using Hamilton's Example as an Illustration, Hamilton's Role and the Nature of Self-Litigation: Essence Over Formalities

Alexander Hamilton's role in the case of People v. Croswell and its implications provides a fascinating and rich illustration. The case of People v. Croswell and Hamilton's involvement is indeed an apt illustration of the importance of focusing on the essence of legal claims over formalities. It also shows how significant legal principles, like freedom of the press, can emerge from cases where the underdog is supported in their fight against more powerful adversaries. However, it's important to note that this example isn't one of pure self-litigation but rather one where the intervention of a skilled lawyer was crucial in achieving a just outcome.

- **Not Purely Self-Litigation:** In the case of People v. Croswell, Harry Croswell initially faced the challenges of self-representation, largely because he lacked the resources to afford a lawyer. However, Alexander Hamilton, a prominent lawyer and former Secretary of the Treasury, took on Croswell's defense pro bono (without charge). While Croswell's situation started as self-litigation due to financial constraints, it shifted when Hamilton stepped in as his advocate. So, while this case involved aspects of self-representation, it ultimately became a significant example of legal advocacy rather than pure self-litigation.

- **Hamilton's Argument:** Hamilton's defense was indeed a powerful example of focusing on the essence of the case over mere formalities. He argued that the truth of the statements made by Croswell in The Wasp should be a valid defense against libel charges, challenging the then-prevailing British legal standards. Hamilton emphasized the fundamental principle that if the statements were true and made with good intentions, they should not be considered libelous, even if they offended those in power.

- **Impact on Legal Doctrine:** This argument was revolutionary because it shifted the focus from procedural technicalities to the substantive truth and intent behind the action. Although the New York Supreme Court did not overturn Croswell's conviction at the time due to a split decision, Hamilton's arguments influenced the New York Legislature to change the law in 1805. This change allowed truth as a defense in libel cases if it was published with good motives, significantly advancing freedom of the speech.

- **Public vs. Private Libel:** Hamilton's distinction between public and private libel further advanced the argument that public figures and businessmen should be subject to greater scrutiny, laying the groundwork for modern understandings of freedom of speech.

Hamilton's defense of Croswell is an excellent example of how the core of a legal claim (the truth and the protection of civil rights) can prevail over strict adherence to formalities. This principle resonates with the idea that in modern legal systems, especially those with provisions for self-representation, courts should focus on the substance of a claim rather than allowing procedural technicalities to obscure justice. While Croswell's case demonstrates that even individuals with limited resources can bring important cases to court, it also highlights the challenges of self-representation. Without Hamilton's intervention, Croswell might not have been able to effectively argue his case, illustrating both the potential and the limitations of self-litigation.

Back to Basics: Singapore as a Model for Government-as-a-Service

My experience and example paints a picture of a legal system that goes beyond mere functionality, aiming to deliver justice in a way that is humane, accessible, and efficient. The broader idea of "government-as-a-service" could revolutionize how public services are delivered globally, making them more responsive, user-friendly, and scalable. Singapore, with its track record of innovation and efficiency, is well-positioned to lead this transformation, potentially setting a new standard for governance as 'metastate'.

Singapore is often cited as a model for efficient and effective governance, particularly in the way it delivers public services. The idea of "government-as-a-service" or "justice-as-a-service" builds on this reputation by suggesting that government functions can be separated from political debate and optimized as scalable, exportable services. Here's how Singapore exemplifies this concept:

1. **User-Centric Approach:** As you've experienced firsthand, Singapore's legal system is designed with the user in mind. The focus on making justice accessible, clear, and convenient—especially for self-represented litigants—demonstrates a commitment to treating citizens as clients who deserve high-quality service. This approach reflects a broader trend in Singapore's public sector, where government agencies strive to deliver services with the efficiency and customer focus typically associated with the private sector.
2. **Digital Integration and Accessibility:** Singapore's embrace of digital tools like the eLitigation system, managed by CrimsonLogic, is a cornerstone of this user-centric approach. By allowing online filings, remote hearings, and direct communication with court staff, the system not only makes the legal process more efficient but also more accessible. This is particularly beneficial for individuals who might otherwise be overwhelmed by the complexity of legal procedures.
3. **Empathy and Support:** The support you received—from CrimsonLogic employees to court registrars—highlights the human element that underpins Singapore's legal system. It's not just about providing a service; it's about ensuring that the service is delivered with empathy, understanding, and a genuine desire to help people navigate what can be a stressful and intimidating process.

4. **Scalability and Exportability:** The idea of scaling Singapore's government services, such as SingPass (the digital identity system) or the justice system, to other countries is a compelling one. These services could potentially be offered to other states or entities as a "government-as-a-service" model, much like software-as-a-service (SaaS) in the tech industry. This could allow other nations or regions to benefit from Singapore's expertise in creating efficient, transparent, and citizen-focused public services without having to build these systems from scratch.

My experience suggests that justice in Singapore is not just about legal outcomes, but about the entire experience of seeking justice. The concept of "justice-as-a-service" would involve:

- **Efficient and Accessible Legal Processes:** Ensuring that legal services are as straightforward and accessible as possible, particularly for those who might not have the resources to hire lawyers.

- **Personalized Support:** Offering tailored assistance to individuals based on their needs, including moral support, clear guidance, and special accommodations for those with disabilities.

- **Digital Platforms and Automation:** Utilizing technology to streamline legal processes, reduce costs, and improve the user experience, all while maintaining the integrity of the legal system.

- **Exportable Legal Services:** Developing models where other countries or regions could adopt these systems, benefiting from Singapore's experience and infrastructure.

Potential Benefits of Using AI in Judicial Decisions

Even now, algorithms are making decisions about loans, and in the future, they want to entrust them with even court cases[7]. We are talking about the very idea of using algorithms to predict people's actions and outcomes. For several years now, the academic community has been actively discussing the use of machine learning to assess and predict this behavior and make very important decisions about their fate based on it. This practice could have far-reaching implications, given how widely machine learning is used today - algorithms based on it are even being proposed for use in courts.

One of the most famous (and radical) examples is a 2017 paper published by a group of scientists led by renowned neural network specialist Jon Kleinberg. According to the authors' calculations, if the decision on whether to release defendants on bail or keep them behind bars until trial were made by algorithms rather than judges, it could reduce the "population" of detention centers by almost 40% without increasing crime rates.

As Kleinberg and his colleagues insisted, this is possible precisely because machine learning is better than a live judge at assessing the personality of the accused and predicting whether they will commit new crimes if their freedom is not restricted before trial. As Kleinberg insisted in one of his many interviews, algorithms can remove the human factor from important decisions and thus make them fairer.

These ideas are still extremely popular among machine learning specialists. Thus, in the last six months alone, several articles have been published on the use of machine learning in assessing the risk of

---

7. https://meduza.io/feature/2024/08/04/uzhe-seychas-resheniya-o-kreditah-prinimayut-algoritmy-a-v-buduschem-im-hotyat-doverit-dazhe-sudebnye-dela

recidivism of convicted criminals, including when making decisions about their possible parole (for example, one and two).

A study by German criminologists led by Sonja Etzler found no significant advantages to using algorithms when trying to understand whether a convicted sex offender would re-offend. Machine learning almost always involves creating models that work on the "black box" principle, where a large set of parameters is fed in and a decision comes out. This is fundamentally different from a human.

When it comes to things like imprisonment - this is a very big problem. After all, we more or less understand what a human judge relies on, but we don't understand what AI is guided by. We simply throw a person into a trained model and get a result. The same models that are trained on human decisions (whether they are about granting loans or assessing the propensity for domestic violence) will inevitably absorb human errors and biases.

The debate surrounding the use of AI algorithms and machine learning in the judicial system and other critical areas of decision-making is both complex and highly consequential. While the potential benefits are significant, so are the risks and ethical concerns.

- **Consistency and Objectivity:** One of the most compelling arguments for using algorithms in judicial decisions is the potential to eliminate human biases and inconsistencies. Unlike human judges, who may be influenced by emotions, fatigue, or unconscious biases, algorithms can apply the same criteria uniformly across all cases.

- **Efficiency and Scale:** Algorithms can process vast amounts of data quickly, making them potentially more efficient than humans in evaluating factors like the risk of re-offending. This could lead to quicker, more data-driven decisions, such as in bail hearings or parole evaluations, possibly reducing overcrowding in prisons.

- **Predictive Accuracy:** Research like that of Jon Kleinberg suggests that algorithms could be better at predicting outcomes, such as whether a defendant will re-offend, by analyzing patterns that may not be obvious to humans. This could lead to better-informed decisions that balance public safety with fairness to the accused.

- **Lack of Transparency (Black Box Problem):** A major concern with machine learning models, especially deep learning models, is their lack of transparency. These models often operate as "black boxes," where the decision-making process is not easily interpretable by humans. This is problematic in judicial settings, where understanding the rationale behind a decision is crucial for fairness and accountability.

- **Bias in Data:** Machine learning algorithms are only as good as the data they are trained on. If the training data includes historical biases—such as racial or socioeconomic disparities in past judicial decisions—the algorithm may perpetuate or even exacerbate these biases. This has been a significant issue in existing predictive policing and criminal justice algorithms, which have sometimes reinforced discriminatory practices.

- **Ethical Concerns:** There are deep ethical implications in entrusting decisions about human freedom to algorithms. Questions arise about the fairness of delegating such responsibility to machines, especially when it comes to high-stakes decisions like sentencing or parole. The use of algorithms could lead to situations where individuals are deprived of liberty based on predictions rather than proven actions.

- **Human Oversight:** One of the most important safeguards against the potential pitfalls of algorithmic decision-making is ensuring that human judges retain oversight. Algorithms should assist, not replace, human judgment, providing recommendations or insights that judges can use in conjunction with their own reasoning.

- **Support and Caution:** While many in the machine learning community advocate for the use of algorithms in judicial settings, there is also a strong voice urging caution. Studies like those by Sonja Etzler indicate that algorithms do not always outperform human judgment and that their effectiveness can vary depending on the context.

- **Hybrid Approaches:** Some suggest that the best way forward may be hybrid systems where algorithms provide recommendations, but human judges make the final decisions. This could combine the strengths of both human intuition and data-driven analysis while mitigating the risks associated with each.

- **Legal and Regulatory Frameworks:** As the use of algorithms in judicial decision-making expands, there will be a growing need for robust legal and regulatory frameworks to ensure transparency, fairness, and accountability. This includes the possibility of requiring explainability in algorithmic decisions and establishing clear standards for their use.

- **Trust in the Legal System:** The introduction of algorithms into the judicial process could affect public trust in the legal system. While some might see it as a move towards more impartial and scientific decision-making, others may view it as dehumanizing or as a loss of accountability.

- **The Role of Technology in Governance:** The debate over algorithms in the courtroom is part of a larger discussion about the role of technology in governance. As governments increasingly rely on technology to make decisions, there will be ongoing tension between efficiency and fairness, between innovation and the preservation of fundamental rights.

The Future of Network States: Pragmatic Optimism and the Art of the Possible

The evolving concepts of network states, delve into some of the most provocative ideas in the intersection of technology, governance, and society. The synthesis of these ideas with historical and philosophical perspectives, such as Thomas More's "Utopia," offers a compelling lens through which to view the potential and challenges of these emerging digital and decentralized forms of governance.

Network states, as proposed by Srinivasan, represent a radical shift in how communities and governance might function in the future. They are, at their core, communities that form around shared values or goals, initially in digital spaces, but with the potential to transition into physical settlements. This model challenges the traditional nation-state, which is often defined by geography, politics, and historical ties, by suggesting that in a digitally connected world, shared beliefs and objectives could be the primary uniting factor.

The idea of "pragmatic optimism" is crucial in this discourse. Unlike utopian idealists or passive pessimists, pragmatic optimists recognize the limitations of current systems but actively work towards incremental improvements. The process of negotiating with governments, drafting policies, and working with various institutions to create new forms of governance is indeed complex and requires a deep understanding of both the possibilities and the constraints of the present systems.

Balaji Srinivasan's argument that technologies like AI and blockchain can both challenge and enhance traditional state functions is particularly relevant. AI's potential to create digital abundance contrasts sharply with blockchain's role in ensuring digital scarcity and authenticity. This dichotomy illustrates how these technologies can be both empowering and destabilizing, depending on how they are implemented and governed.

For instance, AI's ability to democratize services—providing access to virtual lawyers, doctors, and artists—could revolutionize access to basic needs, making them more affordable and widespread. However, this same technology could also create significant challenges in verifying the authenticity of information, a problem that cryptocurrencies and blockchain technology are uniquely positioned to address through decentralized verification systems.

Digital identity and reputation management are key components of the emerging network state infrastructure. These tools are essential for establishing trust and accountability in communities that are not bound by physical proximity or traditional legal frameworks. The development of these technologies could also enable more sophisticated forms of on-chain governance, where decisions are made transparently and democratically, with real-time accountability.

Despite the promise of network states, there are significant challenges and criticisms to consider:

1. **Centralization vs. Decentralization:** Vitalik Buterin's critique of Srinivasan's model highlights a fundamental tension in the concept of network states. While the idea is to decentralize power and create more democratic forms of governance, there is a risk that these communities could replicate the same power structures they seek to escape, with leadership becoming centralized around a few influential figures or entities.
2. **Economic Sustainability:** The financial sustainability of network states remains an open question. Traditional states rely on taxation and other revenue mechanisms to fund public services and infrastructure. Network states will need to develop alternative economic models that can support their communities without relying on traditional state structures.
3. **Legitimacy and Recognition:** Achieving diplomatic recognition is a significant hurdle for network states. Without recognition from existing nation-states, these entities may struggle to establish themselves as legitimate actors in the international arena. This creates a paradox where network states, which seek to transcend traditional governance, must still engage with it to some degree.
4. **Human Psychology and Community Dynamics:** The concept of a network state assumes a level of cohesion and commitment to a shared "one commandment." However, human psychology is complex, and maintaining unity in such communities may prove difficult, especially as they grow larger and more diverse.

As these ideas continue to develop, it will be crucial to monitor how they evolve in practice. The next few years could see the rise of experimental communities that test the boundaries of what is possible with digital governance. These experiments will provide valuable insights into the viability of network states and their potential to offer a real alternative to traditional forms of governance.

The ongoing discussions and projects by figures like Srinivasan, Buterin, and others in the tech and crypto communities are laying the groundwork for these new forms of social organization. Whether these network states can overcome the challenges they face and provide a sustainable, scalable model of governance remains to be seen, but the conversation they have sparked is already influencing how we think about the future of society, technology, and governance.

My own experiences and reflections on Singapore's approach to government services provide a fascinating real-world counterpoint to these theoretical discussions. Singapore's model of efficient, client-oriented public service delivery could offer valuable lessons for the development of network states, particularly in how to balance innovation with practicality and human-centered design.

A man begins to choke in a fancy restaurant.

The waiter rushes over, 'Sir, can I suggest the Heimlich Maneuver?'

The man nods frantically.

The waiter continues, 'Excellent! Shall we pair it with sparkling water or a full-bodied red? ... Also, gratuity is included!'

2. 'Lawyers Herculeses' and ' Hercules the Judge'

'Judge Hercules' to illustrate the theory that judicial decisions should be guided by coherent moral principles, rather than merely following legal rules or precedents[1][3]. These principles have not only legal, but also moral grounds - and 'Hercules the Judge', being not only a jurist, but also a moral philosopher, on the basis of these principles can decide cases even if the law does not tell him what to do. And, fourth, courts should apply the law adequately, and not drag outdated rules into a case just because it is customary. The situation with the fairness of the courts is even more complicated than with their independence.

'Judge Hercules' from Law's Empire

'Judge Hercules' is a hypothetical figure introduced by legal philosopher Ronald Dworkin in his 1986 book Law's Empire[2][4]. This idealized judge possesses superhuman intellect, patience, and legal knowledge, enabling him to interpret and apply the law with perfect consistency and moral integrity. Dworkin uses Judge Hercules to illustrate his theory that judicial decisions should be guided by coherent moral principles, rather than merely following legal rules or precedents.

Very interesting piece by Margarita Bocharova[3] in the Signal[4]: a fair and incorruptible democratic court, an independent court remains a

---

1. https://www.linkedin.com/posts/vsolodkiy_judge-hercules-to-illustrate-the-theory-activity-7265375362782564352-XVoc/
2. https://www.linkedin.com/pulse/fair-trial-utopia-judge-hercules-from-laws-empire-vladislav-solodkiy-t0nte/
3. https://www.linkedin.com/in/margarita-bocharova/

symbol of justice in the last instance. For many people, it is also a necessary component of a good life. (At least, American presidents[5], British politicians[6], representatives of famous political dynasties[7] and historians[8] speak about it.)

A Fair Trial Is A Utopia? *Fair Trial*

- this concept is inscribed[9] in the Universal Declaration of Human Rights. The UN Commission on Human Rights considers[10] a fair trial as one of the most important elements of democracy. Almost everyone agrees that "young democracies" should first of all ensure an independent fair trial (one[11], two[12]). In "old democracies", in turn, the majority of citizens believe[13] that an independent court is more important than, say, succession of power and fair elections.

However, what is a "fair and independent court" is a philosophical question: we all think we know the answer to it, but when we have to formulate it rigorously, it turns out to be unexpectedly difficult.

---

4. https://us10.campaign-archive.com/?e=ba032cae9a&u=ff4a009ba1f59d865f0301f85&id=5dbeb49784

5. https://www.brainyquote.com/quotes/andrew_jackson_401401?src=t_judiciary

6. https://www.brainyquote.com/quotes/david_lidington_1121664?src=t_judiciary

7. https://www.brainyquote.com/quotes/caroline_kennedy_443266?src=t_judiciary

8. https://www.brainyquote.com/quotes/timothy_d_snyder_855177?src=t_judiciary

9. https://www.ohchr.org/ru/universal-declaration-of-human-rights/illustrated-universal-declaration-human-rights

10. https://www.un.org/ru/global-issues/democracy

11. https://www.uscourts.gov/statistics-reports/issue-2-preserving-public-trust-confidence-and-understanding

12. https://www.americanbar.org/groups/judicial/publications/appellate_issues/2023/winter/public-confidence-and-the-courts/

13. https://www.pewresearch.org/global/2019/10/14/democratic-values/

Mexico has decided to[14] elect judges by popular vote in September 2024. The president of the country, who proposed the innovation, stated that it would serve to "strengthen the ideals and principles of humanism, justice, fairness, austerity and democracy".

But exactly the same measure did not work in Bolivia. In theory, the transfer of such a right to citizens should have ensured a belief in fair justice, but in practice the opposite was true. The electability of Bolivian judges led to their politicization, which ultimately undermined citizens' already shaky faith in the rule of law and political stability.

Judicial reforms in Poland in 2019 and in Israel in 2022 were carried out under the banner of judicial independence, and opponents in both cases argued that the reforms actually made the courts more dependent on the ruling parties.

In short, in political rhetoric, an "independent court" is generally a court that doesn't depend on those you don't like; on those you do like, let it depend.

Is There Such a Thing as a Fair and Independent Tribunal?

According to World Bank estimates for[15] 2022, courts operated in a completely non-interventionist environment in Australia. The situation was close to ideal in Norway, Sweden, Finland, Portugal, Ireland, Iceland, Estonia, Austria and the Netherlands.

As in all such indices (corruption, stability, freedom of speech, etc.), it is possible to guess the leaders and outsiders without even looking at

---

14. https://www.mayerbrown.com/en/insights/publications/2024/10/mexicos-controversial-judicial-reform-takes-effect-assessing-its-impact

15. https://prosperitydata360.worldbank.org/en/indicator/IDEA+GSOD+jud_ind_est

the data: the best results will be in the rich Western countries, especially in the Scandinavian countries, and the worst in the Global South. Secular courts are also favored. And that's a big problem.

Independence may be granted individually to each judge or to the judiciary as a whole - how do we know which is better? Or the local demand for justice may at some point require greater government involvement (this happens, for example, in disputes between overly powerful private individuals) - is this good or bad? Finally, courts may balance the public interest in different ways. Some may see this as a manifestation of democracy, while others may see it as a threat to independence.

If judges are completely free from external pressure, how can they be prevented from deciding[16] cases on the basis of personal biases or media publications they have read in their spare time? In the U.S., by the way, this is a common situation: judges of left-wing and right-wing views make different rulings in similar cases, citing different norms and precedents.

The whole system of independent courts is fragile even in the most developed countries. Small mishaps can shake the balance and cause unrest in society (here are a couple of examples: one[17], two[18]). Each country builds[19] its own system of checks and balances: there are regular public reports by representatives of the judiciary, mandatory interaction with journalists, codes of judicial ethics, and so on.

---

16. https://iacajournal.org/articles/10.36745/ijca.528

17. https://www.politico.eu/article/norway-accused-of-meddling-with-judicial-independence-per-christiansen-efta/

18. https://www.kho.fi/fi/index/ajankohtaista/presidentinpuheita/lookinginthemirrortheruleoflawchallengesinfinland.html

19. https://iacajournal.org/issues/29/files/29-90-PB.pdf

The situation with the fairness of the courts is even more complicated than with their independence. People find it difficult to define what justice is, even in the most general sense. Almost 80% of Portuguese perceive[20] justice as an equal distribution of income and wealth among members of society. But in Norway and the Netherlands, more than half of those surveyed disagree with this view. In 2023, an Ipsos survey showed[21] that while in Peru two out of three people agreed that a just society is one of equal opportunity, in India only one in five supported this view, and a further 23% of respondents thought it was more important for justice that all members of society have the same standard of living.

In the US in 2024, the Pew Research Center found[22] that supporters of Donald Trump were twice as likely to expect the justice system to impose harsher sentences on criminals. Among Biden supporters, the majority wanted to leave things as they are or reduce the severity of sentencing. These results suggest very different perceptions of justice.

Back in the middle of the 18th century, the Italian philosopher Cesare Beccaria insisted in his book "On Crimes and Punishments"[23] that the primary function of the justice system is not to restore justice in some higher sense, but a much more modest one: to maintain order and balance in society - most modern legal systems are based on this principle (we have already talked more about it here[24] and here[25]).

---

20. https://www.europeansocialsurvey.org/news/article/justice-and-fairness-analysis-now-available
21. https://www.ipsos.com/sites/default/files/ct/news/documents/2023-07/Ipsos%20-%20Equalities%20Index%202023%20-%20Full%20report.pdf
22. https://www.pewresearch.org/politics/2024/06/06/crime-policing-and-the-2024-election/
23. https://library.nlu.edu.ua/POLN_TEXT/KNIGI-2013/CHezare_Bekkaria_2004.pdf
24. https://us10.campaign-archive.com/?u=ff4a009ba1f59d865f0301f85&id=0cd5e84846
25. https://us10.campaign-archive.com/?u=ff4a009ba1f59d865f0301f85&id=0cd5e84846

This sometimes leads to results that are absurd from the point of view of common sense. For example, stiffer penalties for economic crimes than for violent crimes. The logic here is not quite humanistic: fraud and tax evasion are dangerous not only for a particular person, but also for the "system as a whole". And for a particular person to have a better life, first of all, the smooth functioning of the "system as a whole" is necessary.

A Fair Tribunal is a Utopia too? Partly

But that doesn't mean the concept should be abandoned. The American jurist Ronald Dworkin developed the[26] idea of an ideal infallible judge - a kind of **"Hercules the Lawyer"**. He considered his main strength to be his unlimited knowledge of the principles of law. These principles have not only legal, but also moral grounds - and "Hercules the Judge", being not only a jurist, but also a moral philosopher, on the basis of these principles can decide cases even if the law does not tell him what to do.

Say, a judge in an abstract country needs to decide whether a grandson can receive the inheritance of his grandfather, whom he killed for the sake of this fortune. Technically, there is no barrier to this in the law - after the grandson has served time for murder, of course. But "Judge Hercules" would not let it happen. He would have proceeded on the moral principle that a criminal cannot profit from his crime.

Dworkin believed that a "moral reading" should always be applied to existing law, and that centuries-old laws should be given current-day meaning. In this way, these laws would better meet public demands for justice - and maintain people's faith in their state.

---

26. https://www.youtube.com/watch?v=cCFAxhYa3N4&t=2647s

The problem with such a view is clear: morality is fluid, and there are hardly enough "**Herculean judges**". Nevertheless, society needs faith in abstract, lofty formulas. It is on the basis of values that are sometimes incompatible with reality that people create their identity and feel unity with their colleagues, fellow believers and fellow citizens. But this belief in high values needs something to back it up.

One of the main theorists of justice, the American philosopher John Rawls, insisted[27]: justice can exist in a modern legal system. It would simply be expressed not in terms of balance or truth, but in the form of a correct and impartial use of public rules. He called it 'justice as rightness'.

(The most appropriate punishment for an autocrat would be a fair and incorruptible democratic court - this idea, in general, is not new. In its time, approximately the same demonstrative-democratic trial was organized for the "architect of the Holocaust" Adolf Eichmann (although, beforehand, the Israeli security services stole him from Argentina). The trial was then covered by the[28] correspondent of The New Yorker magazine, philosopher Hannah Arendt. She told the world how Eichmann was burdened and exhausted by the successive and demonstratively independent trials and debates of the parties.)

First, the law should be written in such a way that people have an opportunity to fulfill or not fulfill it. Second, the meaning of norms should be precisely formulated. Third, similar decisions should be

---

27. http://kyiv-heritage-guide.com/sites/default/files/%D0%A0%D0%9E%D0%9B%D0%97%20-%20%D0%A2%D0%B5%D0%BE%D1%80%D0%B8%D1%8F%20%D1%81%D0%BF%D1%80%D0%B0%D0%B2%D0%B5%D0%B4%D0%BB%D0%B8%D0%B2%D0%BE%D1%81%D1%82%D0%B8%D0%BC%201(2010)%20536%D1%81.pdf

28. https://www.forbes.ru/forbes-woman/482773-kak-hanna-arendt-borolas-s-nacizmom-i-pokazala-miru-banal-nost-zla

applied in similar cases. And, fourth, courts should apply the law adequately, and not drag outdated rules into a case just because it is customary.

Without the attainment of such formal justice, Rawls believed that the principles of liberty and equality could not be realized.

How far the real world is from this theoretical construct - this gives rise to public skepticism: people do not believe in justice, nor in a public morality that is one for all. They arbitrarily divide[29] the world into "their own" and "others" - and do not see their fellow citizens as equal in rights and duties. Perhaps it is the belief in "justice as rightness" that can overcome this skepticism - and repoliticize citizens, that is, restore their confidence that their participation matters.

10,000 procedural steps per day is a global standard for Justice: and remember, it's not a destination - it's a Journey! enjoy

It's tricky to pinpoint real-world judges and directly compare them to the hypothetical Hercules, as he

---

29. https://us10.campaign-archive.com/?u=ff4a009ba1f59d865f0301f85&id=1b38a3ea7e

represents an ideal rather than a realistic expectation.

Judge Hercules is not a real person but rather a hypothetical figure created by legal philosopher Ronald Dworkin. He is presented as an idealized judge with superhuman intellectual ability and complete knowledge of the law. Dworkin used Hercules to illustrate his theory of law as integrity, arguing that there is always a single "right answer" to any legal question, and Hercules is capable of finding it. However, we can look for qualities that align with Dworkin's concept:

- **Deep legal knowledge and intellectual rigor:** Judges known for their profound understanding of legal principles, their ability to analyze complex cases, and their contribution to legal scholarship might be considered. In Singapore: Chief Justice Sundaresh Menon is highly regarded for his intellectual depth and contributions to jurisprudence. In the UK: Lord Sumption (now retired) was known for his formidable intellect and scholarly approach to law.

- **Commitment to "law as integrity":** This means striving for coherence and principle within the legal system, looking for solutions that fit with existing laws while upholding fairness and justice. This is harder to assess objectively, as it's about judicial philosophy. Judges who consistently demonstrate a commitment to upholding the rule of law and seeking just outcomes, even in difficult cases, might be seen as embodying this aspect of Hercules.

- **Impartiality and objectivity:** Hercules is unbiased and free from external influences. While no judge is perfectly objective, those with reputations for fairness and independence are closer to this ideal.

It's important to remember that legal systems differ, and what constitutes "Herculean" judgment in Singapore might not be the same as in the UK.

Even the most skilled and ethical judges are human, with limitations and potential biases. Rather than seeking a perfect "Hercules" equivalent, it's more fruitful to look for judges who exemplify key aspects of Dworkin's ideal, contributing to a more just and principled legal system. While no real-life judge can fully embody the idealized "Judge Hercules" concept proposed by Ronald Dworkin, several more judges in Singapore and the United Kingdom have been recognized for their intellectual rigor, moral integrity, and commitment to justice.

- **Justice Philip Jeyaretnam (Singapore):** Appointed as a Judicial Commissioner of the Supreme Court of Singapore in January 2021 and as a Judge in November 2021, Justice Jeyaretnam has been noted for his expertise in arbitration, construction law, and litigation. He received the C.C. Tan Award from the Law Society of Singapore in 2020, which honors lawyers who exemplify the Bar's traditions of integrity, fairness, and gentlemanly conduct.

- **Justice Lai Kew Chai (Singapore):** Serving as a High Court judge from 1981 until his passing in 2006, Justice Lai was involved in several landmark cases. He was known for his meticulous judgments and dedication to upholding the rule of law.

- **Baroness Brenda Hale (United Kingdom):** As the first female President of the Supreme Court of the United Kingdom, Baroness Hale has been celebrated for her contributions to family law and human rights. Her judgments often reflect a deep commitment to justice and equality.

- **Lord David Neuberger (United Kingdom):** Serving as President of the Supreme Court from 2012 to 2017, Lord Neuberger was recognized for his intellectual depth and fair-mindedness. He has also contributed to discussions on judicial ethics and the importance of moral courage in the judiciary.

These judges exemplify qualities akin to Dworkin's "Judge Hercules" through their dedication to legal principles, moral reasoning, and the pursuit of justice.

Here are some notable cases involving Justice Philip Jeyaretnam and Baroness Brenda Hale:

- **ByBit Fintech Ltd v Ho Kai Xin and others [2023] SGHC 199:** In this landmark decision, Justice Jeyaretnam addressed the legal status of cryptocurrency assets. He ruled that crypto assets, such as the stablecoin Tether, are considered "things in action," granting them legally enforceable property rights. This judgment has significant implications for the treatment of digital assets under Singaporean law.

- **Mah Kiat Seng v Attorney-General [2022] SGHC 200:** Justice Jeyaretnam presided over a case where Mr. Mah sued the police for unlawful arrest under the Mental Health (Care and Treatment) Act. The court found that the arresting officer fabricated observations to justify the apprehension, leading to Mr. Mah being awarded $20,000 in damages. This case underscores the judiciary's role in upholding individual rights against unlawful state actions.

- **R (Miller) v The Prime Minister [2019] UKSC 41:** In a historic ruling, the UK Supreme Court, led by Baroness Hale, declared Prime Minister Boris Johnson's advice to prorogue Parliament unlawful. The court held that the suspension had the effect of frustrating or preventing the ability of Parliament to carry out its constitutional functions without reasonable justification. This decision reinforced the principle of parliamentary sovereignty and the limits of executive power.

- **Stack v Dowden [2007] UKHL 17:** Baroness Hale delivered a leading judgment in this case concerning the division of property between cohabiting partners. She emphasized that in the absence of explicit agreements, courts should consider the entire course of conduct between parties to determine their respective shares. This approach marked a significant development in family property law, focusing on fairness and the realities of modern relationships.

These cases illustrate how both judges have shaped legal principles and protected individual rights through their thoughtful and impactful judgments.

However, attributing judgments entirely to a judge's individual "Herculean" qualities is difficult, as judgments are often shaped by legal teams, precedents, and the specifics of the case. That said, here are few more examples where judges demonstrated qualities reminiscent of Judge Hercules:

- **Chief Justice Sundaresh Menon in Hii Chii Kok v Ooi Peng Jin London Lucien and another (2017, Singapore):** This case dealt with complex questions about the law of trusts and fiduciary duties. CJ Menon's judgment was praised for its clarity, rigorous analysis of legal principles, and its effort to create a coherent framework for understanding these complex areas of law. This aligns with Hercules' ability to find the "right answer" through deep legal understanding.

- **Lord Sumption in Prest v Petrodel Resources Ltd and others (2013, UK):** This case involved intricate company law issues and the "piercing the corporate veil" doctrine. Lord Sumption's judgment provided a comprehensive analysis of this doctrine, clarifying its scope and application. This demonstrates his intellectual rigor and commitment to legal coherence, key traits of Dworkin's Hercules.

It's important to note that these examples highlight specific aspects of "Herculean" judging, not a perfect embodiment.

Finding a single judgment that perfectly encapsulates all of Hercules' qualities is unlikely. It's interesting to consider whether "Herculean" judging, as inspired by Dworkin's ideal, might be more prevalent in certain legal systems. There are factors that could influence this:

Factors that might favor "Herculean" judging in the USA:

- **Strong emphasis on individual rights:** The US legal system places a high value on individual rights and liberties, often leading to complex legal arguments and a need for judges to balance competing interests. This could encourage judges to delve deeply into legal principles and strive for nuanced interpretations, similar to Hercules' pursuit of the "right answer."

- **Common law system:** The US, like the UK, relies on a common law system where judicial precedent plays a crucial role. This requires judges to engage in extensive analysis of past cases and legal doctrines, potentially fostering a more "Herculean" approach.

- **Judicial review:** The US Supreme Court's power of judicial review allows it to strike down laws deemed unconstitutional. This places a significant burden on judges to interpret the Constitution and weigh fundamental principles, potentially demanding a high degree of intellectual rigor.

Factors that might make "Herculean" judging less pronounced in Singapore:

- **Emphasis on efficiency and pragmatism:** Singapore's legal system, while based on common law, also emphasizes efficiency and pragmatism. This might sometimes prioritize clear and practical solutions over highly nuanced or theoretical legal arguments.

- **Less adversarial system:** While Singapore has an adversarial system, it may be less adversarial than the US. This could lead to less emphasis on elaborate legal arguments and a greater focus on finding mutually agreeable solutions.

- **Stronger executive branch:** The executive branch in Singapore generally plays a more prominent role compared to the US. This might lead to less emphasis on judicial activism and a more restrained approach to judicial decision-making.

- **These are generalizations:** Individual judges and specific cases can vary greatly within any legal system.

Many other countries, such as those in Europe with strong civil law traditions, could also exhibit "Herculean" judging in different ways. The nature of judging is constantly evolving, and factors like globalization and technological advancements can influence judicial approaches across different countries.

- A woman calls 911. "My house is on fire!"
- "Please state the nature of your emergency."
- "I just did! Seeeend help!"
- "Ma'am, I need to fill out the 'Emergency Details' section completely."

Ultimately, while certain legal systems might provide a more conducive environment for "Herculean" judging, the individual qualities and commitment of judges themselves remain the most crucial factor.

It is fair to say that judicial behavior resembling "Judge Hercules"—defined by a commitment to broad moral reasoning, individual rights, and interpreting law in ways that create significant societal impact—may be perceived as more common in the United States compared to countries like Singapore or the UK. This difference arises from distinct legal traditions, cultural contexts, and institutional structure:

1. Judicial Philosophy and Role:

- United States: Judges, particularly at the Supreme Court level, often adopt activist roles where they are expected to interpret the Constitution in ways that address broad societal issues (e.g., Roe v. Wade, Brown v. Board of Education). This aligns with the idea of a judge who integrates moral reasoning with legal interpretation.

- Singapore and UK: Judges typically embrace a more restrained approach, focusing on interpreting and applying existing laws without venturing into activism. Singapore's judiciary, in particular, emphasizes pragmatic and technocratic approaches over ideological debates.

2. Constitutional Framework:

- United States: A written constitution and a strong emphasis on judicial review provide greater scope for judges to address fundamental rights and principles.

- Singapore: Judicial review exists but is more narrowly defined, with judges emphasizing the rule of law and deferring to legislative intent unless clear violations of law occur. The UK, while having an unwritten constitution, also leans towards judicial restraint, although cases like Miller v. Prime Minister (led by Baroness Hale) show moments of judicial assertiveness.

3. Cultural Context and Judicial Independence:

- United States: A strong tradition of individualism and public scrutiny encourages judges to take bold stances. Lifetime appointments for Supreme Court justices further enable them to act with relative independence.

- Singapore: Judges operate within a framework that prioritizes stability, economic development, and deference to the executive branch. Judicial decisions tend to align with broader societal goals rather than challenge them dramatically.

- UK: Judges maintain independence but often navigate a balance between deference to Parliament (sovereignty of Parliament is a core principle) and upholding the rule of law.

4. Case Law and Precedent:

- United States: Judges frequently create landmark rulings that set new precedents, influencing law and society directly.

- Singapore and UK: Precedent plays a key role, and significant changes often emerge gradually or through legislative action rather than judicial intervention.

The perception that "Herculean" judicial behavior is more common in the U.S. is largely accurate,

driven by the nation's constitutional framework, cultural expectations, and judiciary's role in shaping public policy. In contrast, Singapore and the UK lean towards judicial restraint, with exceptions in cases of high public or constitutional significance.

- In the U.S., cases with dramatic implications (e.g., civil rights, abortion, gun laws) often receive extensive media coverage, reinforcing the image of judicial boldness.

- In Singapore, the judiciary is seen as an arbiter of disputes and a stabilizing institution rather than a driver of social change.

The UK judiciary occasionally demonstrates activism (as in Miller), but it is more restrained compared to its American counterpart.

"Your Honor," the defendant cries, "I'm being buried under lawsuits! They owe me money, yet they use their wealth to drown me in legal procedures!"
The judge adjusts his wig. "Order! Order!, kindly remind the defendant that justice is blind, but it's not deaf to improperly formatted footnotes. Now, let's discuss the precise kerning of your submissions... Failure to comply may result in contempt of court charges!"

3. The Paradox of Self-Representation: Advancing Fairness in Legal Systems

The cornerstone of any just society is a legal system that upholds fairness and equality before the law. In Singapore, renowned for its robust legal framework, a critical question arises: Is it fair to compensate only the legal costs incurred from professional lawyers when a party wins or settles a case in court or through mediation? This question gains urgency when considering individuals who, due to financial constraints imposed by their opponents, are compelled to represent themselves against well-resourced adversaries.

The Predicament of Self-Representation

Self-representation is often not a choice but a necessity forced upon individuals by circumstances beyond their control. Imagine facing a wealthy and influential opponent who strategically depletes your financial resources — keeping you "without money" — and consequently, without the means to hire professional legal representation. This tactic not only strips you of legal counsel but also burdens you with the complexities of navigating the legal system alone.

Adding insult to injury, such opponents may then criticize you for choosing self-representation, arguing that you should have hired a lawyer. Meanwhile, they accumulate exorbitant legal fees, which are deemed fair and compensable simply because they are expenses billed by professional lawyers. Your request to be compensated for your time and effort in defending yourself is dismissed as unfair. This scenario raises profound questions about the equity of the legal process.

The Disparity in Legal Cost Compensation: A Call for Fairness in (Singapore's) Judicial System

The current practice in Singapore's courts, which compensates only for professional legal costs, creates a significant disparity. It inherently values the time and expertise of professional lawyers over the substantial effort and time invested by self-represented litigants. This disparity is especially stark when the opponent's legal expenses far exceed the amount in dispute or the potential reward.

- A man thrashes in a lake, shouting, "Help! I can't swim!"
- A passerby in a suit responds, "Do you have a permit for aquatic distress?"
- "Permit? I'm drowning!"
- Well, without the proper paperwork, assisting you would violate several regulations. Perhaps you should consult the Manual of Water Emergencies!

16 Landmark Cases on Legal Cost Compensation: Insights from Five Jurisdictions[1][5]

Internationally, courts in jurisdictions with common law traditions — such as England, Australia, Canada, and the United States — have

---

1. https://medium.com/@slavasolodkiy/the-paradox-of-self-representation-advancing-fairness-in-legal-systems-03ae06418b6f

grappled with similar issues. In some cases, courts have recognized the need to compensate self-represented litigants under exceptional circumstances, especially when they were forced into self-representation due to the actions of their opponents.

International Precedents and Principles

Several cases (16 Cases from Five Jurisdictions below) illustrate this evolving recognition for example:

1. Cachia v Hanes (1994) — Australia
2. Oshlack v Richmond River Council (1998) — Australia
3. Moorview Developments Ltd v First Active Plc (2010) — Ireland
4. Kay v Ehrler (1991) — The U.S. Supreme Court
5. Re Elgindata Ltd (No 2) (1992) — England

These cases, among others (eleven more below), demonstrate a judicial willingness to consider the unique circumstances of self-represented litigants, especially when fairness and access to justice are at stake.

Ethical and Legal Implications

From an ethical standpoint, compensating only professional legal costs undermines the principle of equality before the law. It places individuals without financial means at a significant disadvantage, effectively penalizing them for their inability to afford professional representation. This practice raises concerns about access to justice — a fundamental right in any democratic society.

Moreover, when wealthy opponents employ strategies to financially incapacitate their adversaries, they exploit a systemic vulnerability.

Such tactics not only disadvantage the individual but also burden the judicial system with protracted litigation that could have been avoided.

Towards a Fairer Legal System

Addressing these disparities requires a reevaluation of the policies governing legal cost compensation in Singapore. Several steps could be taken:

- **Recognizing Exceptional Circumstances:** Courts could adopt a more flexible approach by considering whether a self-represented litigant was forced into that position due to the opponent's actions. If so, compensating them for their time and effort would promote fairness.

- **Emphasizing Real Financial Costs:** Allowing self-represented litigants to recover actual expenses incurred, such as costs for research, document preparation, and expert consultations, acknowledges their contributions and expenses.

- **Public Interest Considerations:** In cases where the litigant's actions serve a broader public interest, courts could recognize the societal value of their efforts by compensating their costs.

- **Preventing Abuse of Process:** Implementing safeguards against opponents who misuse legal procedures to financially drain their adversaries would protect the integrity of the judicial process.

Justice must be accessible and equitable, not a privilege afforded only to those with substantial resources. The fairness of compensating only professional legal costs in Singapore's courts deserves critical examination. By acknowledging the challenges faced by self-represented litigants and valuing their time and effort, the legal system can uphold its commitment to justice for all.

International precedents provide valuable insights into how courts can navigate these complex issues. Incorporating such considerations into Singapore's legal framework would not only enhance fairness but also reinforce the nation's dedication to the rule of law and equal justice.

It is imperative that the legal system evolves to address these disparities, ensuring that every individual, regardless of financial standing, can engage with the judicial process on fair terms. Justice should not only be done but should manifestly be seen to be done — fairly and without prejudice.

Is it Fair to Compensate Only Legal Costs in (Singaporean) Courts?

For sure, it is not so inspiring, visionary and forwardthinking question as 'To sue or not to sue'[2]. The concept of justice, particularly in the context of legal cost compensation, goes beyond financial transactions. It reflects the societal values of fairness, accessibility, and accountability. In Singaporean courts, where the principle is to compensate the prevailing party's legal costs, a question arises: Is it truly fair when this system excludes the time, effort, and sacrifices made by self-represented litigants?

The argument often made in defense of this system is that professional lawyers' fees represent an industry standard. Their expertise is recognized and valued. However, does this logic hold when the self-litigant achieves similar or better outcomes, often under immense pressure?

---

2. https://singaporelitigationlawyer.com/author/singaporelitigationlawyer/page/2/

To deny a self-litigant compensation for their time while rewarding their opponents' expensive lawyers creates a paradox: a justice system that penalizes the underprivileged for their ingenuity and resilience. True justice acknowledges the efforts of those who fight for their rights, often against overwhelming odds, and ensures that fairness extends beyond those who can afford professional representation.

Examples of 16 Legal Cases (England, Ireland, Canada, USA, Australia)

These cases collectively demonstrate that courts across jurisdictions have recognized the need for fairness when financial limitations or opponent misconduct forces self-representation. They pave the way for broader arguments about compensating self-litigants for their time, effort, and incurred expenses, creating a foundation for reform.

1. **Cachia v. Hanes (1994) 179 CLR 403 (Australia):**

The High Court of Australia ruled that a party compelled to represent themselves due to the opponent's misconduct may be entitled to compensation for their efforts. This closely parallels cases where individuals are forced into self-representation because of financial constraints created by their opponents.

2. **Oshlack v. Richmond River Council [1998] HCA 11 (Australia):**

The High Court of Australia recognized that in exceptional circumstances, where a party acts in the public interest and without personal gain, they may be exempted from reimbursing the opposing side's legal costs. While this case is about waiving cost obligations, it demonstrates the court's willingness to deviate from standard rules in unique situations.

3. **Moorview Developments Ltd v. First Active Plc [2010] IEHC 275 (Ireland):**

The court allowed cost compensation to a self-represented litigant when their time and effort were deemed critical and justified for the case. Despite lacking formal legal counsel, the plaintiff faced significant financial burden due to circumstances beyond their control.

4. **Kidd v. Pan American World Airways Inc. (1990) CanLII 5787 (Canada):**

In Canada, the court awarded compensation to a self-represented litigant after establishing that the defendant deliberately delayed the proceedings, significantly increasing the plaintiff's costs.

5. **New Brunswick (Minister of Health) v. G(J) [1999] 3 SCR 46 (Canada):**

The Supreme Court of Canada held that denial of legal assistance could violate the right to a fair trial under the Canadian Charter of Rights and Freedoms, framing legal aid as a fundamental right.

6. **Okanagan Indian Band v. British Columbia [2003] 3 SCR 371 (Canada):**

The Supreme Court of Canada permitted a self-represented litigant to claim legal costs, citing public interest and the plaintiff's financial inability to afford counsel.

7. Re Elgindata Ltd (No 2) [1992] 1 WLR 1207 (England):

This case affirmed that self-represented litigants could seek reimbursement for real financial losses, such as costs for expert consultants, even if they did not engage formal legal counsel.

8. Donoghue v. Stevenson [1932] UKHL 100 (England):

A landmark case on fairness and due care, it indirectly supports claims that opponents who delay or obstruct justice cause significant harm to the aggrieved party.

9. McKenzie v. McKenzie [1971] P 33 (England):

The court introduced the concept of "McKenzie friends," emphasizing the importance of supporting self-represented litigants to ensure they receive fair assistance despite financial limitations.

10. R v. Lord Chancellor, ex parte Lightfoot [2000] QB 597 (England):

This case highlighted that financial constraints should not impede the right to a fair trial. It reinforces arguments against systemic barriers caused by opponents' actions.

11. London Scottish Benefit Society v. Chorley [1884] 13 QBD 872 (England):

Recognized the right of self-represented parties to recover costs for their time and effort during litigation. This ruling underscores the importance of valuing the contributions of those forced into self-representation.

12. **Kay v. Ehrler, 499 U.S. 432 (1991) (USA):**

The U.S. Supreme Court ruled that an attorney representing themselves cannot claim legal fees under the Civil Rights Act. However, the court emphasized the purpose of cost recovery is to encourage hiring qualified counsel — a point that underscores how opponents' actions often deprive self-represented litigants of such options.

13. **Carter v. Veterans Administration, 780 F.2d 1479 (9th Cir. 1986) (USA):**

The Ninth Circuit Court of Appeals noted that while self-represented litigants cannot claim attorney fees, they may recover other legal costs incurred during litigation. This principle is critical when addressing significant expenses borne during self-defense.

14. **Richlin Security Service Co. v. Chertoff, 553 U.S. 571 (2008) (USA):**

The U.S. Supreme Court ruled that victorious parties could claim costs for paralegals under the Equal Access to Justice Act. This precedent supports compensation for expenses on consultants or experts engaged in lieu of formal legal representation.

15. **Brewer v. McEwen (1988) 197 Cal.App.3d 358 (USA):**

A California court awarded cost recovery to a self-represented litigant when the opposing party's bad faith actions forced them to represent themselves. This precedent is powerful when proving intentional delays or financial obstruction by opponents.

16. Case Management by Non-Lawyers (USA):

U.S. courts, especially in bankruptcy or consumer protection cases, have awarded cost compensation to self-represented litigants who could prove financial limitations prevented hiring an attorney and that they incurred substantial losses as a result of representing themselves.

- **Kay v. Ehrler, 499 U.S. 432 (1991):** The U.S. Supreme Court ruled that a lawyer representing themselves cannot recover attorney fees under the Civil Rights Act. The rationale was that the purpose of fee-shifting statutes is to incentivize hiring qualified counsel. Usefulness for Non-Lawyers: (While this case is not directly helpful for non-lawyers because it focuses on attorneys representing themselves. However,) the judgment's reasoning about incentivizing qualified legal representation can be reframed. For instance, you could argue that your lack of representation was not a choice but a necessity caused by the opposing party's financial tactics. This aligns with the intent of fee-shifting statutes: ensuring fairness when external factors prevent access to legal counsel.

- **Carter v. Veterans Administration, 780 F.2d 1479 (9th Cir. 1986):** The Ninth Circuit ruled that self-represented litigants cannot claim attorney fees under the Equal Employment Opportunity Act but may recover other litigation costs incurred during the case. Usefulness for Non-Lawyers: This case is relevant for non-lawyers as it establishes that non-attorney pro se litigants can recover certain litigation costs beyond attorney fees. If you've incurred significant costs, such as filing fees, copying expenses, or fees for experts, this precedent can support your claim for reimbursement of those expenses.

- **Richlin Security Service Co. v. Chertoff, 553 U.S. 571 (2008):** The U.S. Supreme Court allowed the successful party to recover paralegal costs under the Equal Access to Justice Act, suggesting that compensation extends beyond attorney fees. Usefulness for Non-Lawyers: This case is very useful for non-lawyers. It broadens the scope of compensable costs to include professional assistance (e.g., consultants or paralegals). If you relied on external experts, advisors, or document preparation services while self-representing, this precedent can help justify claims for those expenses as essential for your case.

Instead of relying heavily on these three last US cases (№16), focus on the Australian and Canadian cases: These cases, particularly Cachia v Hanes, Oshlack v Richmond River Council, Moorview Developments Ltd v First Active Plc, Kidd v. Pan American World Airways Inc., and Okanagan Indian Band v. British Columbia, provide stronger arguments as they directly address self-represented litigants and the potential for compensating their time and effort. Frame your argument around the fundamental right to access justice, emphasizing that denying compensation for a self-represented litigant's time solely due to their lack of formal legal credentials contradicts the principles of fairness and equity inherent in the legal system. Highlight how your invested time warrants recognition and compensation as a matter of justice.

The question is not merely whether the current system is fair but whether it aligns with the core principles of justice we seek to uphold. It's time for Singaporean courts — and courts globally — to take a stand for equity in the courtroom.

The ship is sinking, and a passenger bursts into the captain's cabin.
The captain looks up, 'Sorry, I only deal with iceberg complaints on Tuesdays.'

My own experiences navigating the Singaporean legal system

When I moved to Singapore in May 2015, my friends, well-acquainted with my penchant for supporting the underdog and challenging the status quo, were perplexed. "How will you survive?" they'd ask, "There's no opposition there!" They were right. There wasn't, and perhaps there needn't be.

In a place where the state actively seeks feedback at every turn, where citizen input is not just welcomed but actively sought, the very concept of "opposition" takes on a different meaning. Why protest for the sake of protest when you can simply suggest improvements? The Singaporean government, in my experience, doesn't bristle at criticism. Instead, it embraces practical suggestions as opportunities for growth and refinement.

This is because the state in Singapore functions as a service provider, expertly separated from the realm of politics. Efficiency, convenience, and customer satisfaction are paramount. You feel like a valued customer, not a subject. The message is clear: the state thrives when its people thrive. This creates a symbiotic relationship where individual success contributes to the collective good, and the state, in turn, facilitates that success.

While Singaporeans are known for their respect for rules and procedures, there's a refreshing pragmatism at play. Rules, they acknowledge, are reflections of the past, while progress necessitates embracing the unknown future. This isn't to say rules are disregarded, but rather that they are seen as adaptable guidelines, subject to change as circumstances evolve.

My own experiences navigating the Singaporean legal system as both defendant and claimant have further illuminated this unique approach. While I've previously lauded the efficiency of the online court system (I've already written a lot about the pros—for example, here[3][6]), there are areas ripe for improvement[4][7].

---

3. https://www.linkedin.com/pulse/online-court-singapore-justice-as-a-service-new-vladislav-solodkiy-my6je/

4. https://l.nansen.id/eLetigation

The eLitigation system, for instance, is inaccessible to self-litigants, seemingly pushing individuals to hire legal representation. While understandable from a security and efficiency standpoint, this creates an unnecessary barrier to justice. Why not allow law firms to act as intermediaries for document submission, ensuring quality control while empowering individuals?

Furthermore, the process is riddled with bureaucratic hurdles: repetitive KYC procedures, lack of SingPass integration, manual data entry by CrimsonLogic officers, and the inability to authorize representatives for document submission all contribute to unnecessary delays and frustration.

While I appreciate the value of in-person hearings, the insistence on physical appearances for purely procedural matters seems like a waste of time and resources in the age of online communication. Similarly, the requirement for physical certification of documents, despite the widespread adoption of e-signatures, feels archaic.

The lack of a centralized online platform for case tracking, document access, and important dates further exacerbates the challenges faced by self-litigants, especially when facing opponents who weaponize bureaucracy.

These frustrations are compounded by the occasional rigid adherence to procedure over substance. Whether it's the insistence on a specific type of medical certificate for court absence or the dismissal of logical inconsistencies in opponents' arguments as mere "opinions," the focus on process can sometimes overshadow the pursuit of justice.

Despite these challenges, my experience has been significantly aided by the rise of AI tools like ChatGPT and Gemini. These technologies have been invaluable in navigating the complexities of the legal system, reminding me to "ask the right questions" and empowering me to advocate for myself effectively.

In conclusion, Singapore's unique approach to governance, with its emphasis on citizen feedback, efficient service delivery, and adaptable rules, creates an environment where progress and harmony coexist. While the legal system presents its own set of challenges, particularly for self-litigants, the potential for improvement is undeniable. By embracing technology, streamlining procedures, and prioritizing substance over blind adherence to process, Singapore can further enhance its already impressive system and ensure access to justice for all.

- We need an ambulance!
- Certainly. Have you filled out the Emergency Assistance Application?

Dedicated to the esteemed legal professionals of Singapore, who uphold the highest standards of justice, ethics, and the spirit of the law.

Part 2: Justice Decoded: Navigating the Legal Maze with AI

Leveling the Legal Playing Field: ***AI, Self-Litigation****, and the Quest for a Fairer System*

> An office worker notices flames licking at the edges of a filing cabinet. "Fire! Someone call for help!"
> The manager looks up calmly. "Did you submit a requisition form for emergency services?"
> "Whaat?! The building is on fire!"
> "Procedures exist for a reason," the manager says, adjusting his tie. "Let's not act rashly."

4. How I Took on Seven Top Expensive Lawyers Armed with Just ChatGPT (and a Truth)

They said it couldn't be done[5][8]. They said that obtaining a U.S. banking license as a non-American was a quest best left to the quixotic. "It's incredibly complex," they warned. "Only the most seasoned professionals can navigate that labyrinth." Yet, armed with

---
5. https://www.linkedin.com/pulse/how-i-took-seven-top-expensive-lawyers-armed-just-chatgpt-solodkiy-ntf5e/

determination (and perhaps a dash of naivety), I did it. Little did I know that this adventure would be the prelude to an even more audacious endeavor: representing myself against seven high-powered lawyers in Singapore, with only ChatGPT by my side.

Yes, you read that correctly. Seven lawyers. Me. And an AI language model available for $20 a month. If this were a David versus Goliath tale, even David might have advised me to consider a less confrontational hobby.

The Unlikely Alliance

In the beginning, there were lawyers—my lawyers—defending me in a Singaporean lawsuit in 2023 and early 2024. But as the plot thickened, it became clear that traditional legal counsel was, shall we say, not delivering the riveting performance I had hoped for. Enter ChatGPT, stage right.

With the AI's help (let's be honest, ChatGPT did 99% of the heavy lifting), we filed our own lawsuits in Singapore in July 2024 (District and Magistrate Courts). Not content with merely juggling four cases in State Courts, we threw in HC 618 (Supreme Courts) in August for good measure. Because why fight one battle when you can fight five (seven - but two more are under NDA) simultaneously?

Crafting the Magnum Opus

Together, we penned four Affidavits of Evidence-in-Chief (AEICs). The pièce de résistance was, in my humble opinion, my poems about Her Majesty Logic ("The most powerful questions lead to the most powerful answers"), history of Lord Justice and Sir Self-Litigation for esteemed lawyers. They were documents so compelling that they might just replace bedtime stories for law students worldwide.

We responded to every claim from the defendants' attorneys with a blend of bravado, confidence, and razor-sharp argumentation. The exchanges were so gripping that they could be compiled into a legal thriller (sharing now step-by-step via Linkedin and Medium) — and coming soon to a bookstore near you.

The Art of the (Virtual) Inquiry with a Punch

During the Arival AGM in July and August 2024, ChatGPT and I became quite the investigative duo. We delved into the enigmatic backgrounds of Vladimir Polyakov and Shukur Israilov, unearthing connections that would make a conspiracy theorist blush. ENRC, Roscongress, Paradise Papers, war in Ukraine and demand for high-risk banking, Putin circle behaviour pattern, Wirecard and Marsalek experience, sapphire and defence, sanctions—you name it, we questioned it. We peppered them, the companies, fellow shareholders, and directors with inquiries. Our questions were as relentless as they were incisive, shining a light into the dimmest corners of corporate opacity.

With the AI's eloquent assistance, I authored a couple of blog posts. The first dissected the defendants' penchant for, shall we say, "fiscal reticence" and wove a narrative connecting their behavior to a broader pattern of strategic nonpayment. The second untangled the web of confusion surrounding the three (who knows, maybe more?) Vladimir Polyakovs—it's like a Russian nesting doll of intrigue.

We didn't stop there. Hot off the presses from The Guardian's investigation into ENRC, we crafted a third, searing exposé on Shukur Israilov. Although not mentioned in the investigation (details, details), the timing was impeccable. We drew parallels that were as bold as they were, admittedly, speculative.

Courtroom Antics and Legal Acrobatics

The first hearings for State Courts' cases unfolded in Singapore. Against all odds, and perhaps the laws of conventional jurisprudence, things went quite well. So well, in fact, that I began to wonder if the five (now - seven!) opposing lawyers were starting to question their career choices. Following the hearings, the release of The Guardian's investigation felt like a cosmic wink. We seized the moment, penning a persuasive letter to the court to highlight this fresh off the press revelation. It was a masterstroke of timing and tenacity.

Most of the work I've done with ChatGPT, but over recent months Gemini improved so well to become my second 'partner-in-crime'.

This Wednesday, we had our first session for HC 618 in the High Court. Once again, ChatGPT proved to be the silent partner every self-represented litigant dreams of. We navigated the complexities of the High Court with a blend of audacity and a perhaps misplaced sense of invincibility.

Reflections on an Unorthodox Journey: The Irony of Expertise

Looking back, it's clear that this journey has been anything but ordinary. From challenging the norms of the U.S. banking establishment to taking on a small army of legal professionals, the path has been winding and fraught with skepticism from onlookers.

Yet, throughout this odyssey, ChatGPT has been more than a tool; it's been a confidant, a strategist, and occasionally, a therapist. Who would have thought that an AI language model could exhibit more empathy and reliability than many of its human counterparts?

There's a certain irony in being told that only "super-professionals" can accomplish tasks that, with the right resources and determination, are entirely within reach. It's almost as if the gatekeepers have a vested interest in maintaining the mystique of their domains. But as we've shown, the walls of convention are more like curtains—easily parted with a bit of curiosity and a helpful AI.

A Word on Human Nature: When AI is more Human

Throughout this saga, I've learned that when the going gets tough, people often get...going—in the opposite direction. Colleagues and friends who might have been expected to stand firm tended to waver, offering lukewarm support at best. But it doesn't matter. With ChatGPT, I had an ally that didn't flinch, tire, or second-guess our mission.

So here we are, still standing, still fighting, and perhaps even turning the tide. Armed with nothing more than an AI subscription and an unwillingness to accept "that's just how it's done," we've managed to make a dent in the formidable facade of legal bureaucracy.

To anyone told that they can't achieve something because it's "too complicated" or reserved for the elite few, I offer this piece of advice: question everything, embrace unorthodoxy, and don't underestimate the power of a well-crafted argument—especially one polished by artificial intelligence.

After all, in a world where seven lawyers can be challenged by one person with a laptop and a penchant for asking the right questions, perhaps the impossible isn't so unattainable after all.

And welcome to the Legal Olympics!!!
Today's event: Form-Filing Freestyle! Contestants will be judged on speed, accuracy, and adherence to obscure regulations.
The grand prize?! A 5-minute hearing to discuss the actual merits of your case!!!

A Compendium of Curious Cogitation: Or, How Not to Argue with a Stickler for Syllogisms

It appears my esteemed opponents, despite wielding the formidable legal artillery of Rajah & Tann, occasionally stumble on the battlefield of logic. Their forays into the realm of reason, while valiant, sometimes resemble a drunken tightrope walker attempting a triple somersault – ambitious, but ultimately destined for a faceplant. Allow me to present a catalogue of these "logic gaps," as observed through the lens of yours truly, a connoisseur of coherent argumentation.

The Case of the Vanishing Premise (15 August 2024)

In one of their letters, a masterpiece of legal obfuscation, they construct an argument akin to a magic trick. A premise disappears! Poof! Gone! Leaving us with a conclusion hanging in mid-air like a misplaced modifier. As I so eloquently pointed out to one of R&T lawyers, "if you break the statement into a formula, you see that we're either dealing with a judgment with a missing premise or with an 'implied' (omitted) conclusion." Perhaps they assumed I wouldn't notice? Or maybe they misplaced it along with their common sense.

The "Consulting Agreements" Conundrum (27 September 2024)

Ah, the infamous attempt to conflate unrelated proceedings based on the mere mention of "consulting agreements." This, my friends, is akin to claiming that all cases involving the word "contract" are intrinsically linked. One might as well argue that all cases mentioning the word "money" should be heard in the same court, regardless of whether it involves a parking ticket or international embezzlement. The Judiciary, bless their souls, were not swayed by this dazzling display of legal legerdemain.

The "Irrelevant Noise" Symphony (13 November 2024)

Another R&T lawyer, in his infinite wisdom, bombarded me with a barrage of questions, seemingly designed to test the limits of human patience rather than elicit relevant information. Faced with this onslaught of incoherence, I was forced to issue an ultimatum: "Either you clarify the relevance of each question to the essence of the case, or I will ignore them as irrelevant noise that distracts from the issues at hand and simply wastes everyone's time." Alas, my plea for clarity fell on deaf ears, or perhaps ears clogged with irrelevant legal jargon.

The "Intrinsic Tie" Tango (26 September 2024)

In their quest to delay the inevitable, R&T performed a dazzling dance around the concept of an "intrinsic tie" between one claim and the ongoing another case. This "tie," upon closer inspection, appears to be woven from the flimsiest of threads, more akin to a cobweb than a sturdy rope. One can only admire their audacity in attempting to pass off such gossamer connections as a legitimate basis for a stay of proceedings.

While I applaud my opponents' creativity in constructing these elaborate logical labyrinths, I must, alas, deduct points for coherence and soundness. Perhaps a refresher course in basic logic is in order? I hear there are some excellent textbooks available. Or, if they prefer a more interactive approach, I'm always happy to provide a personalized tutorial on the art of constructing a valid argument. After all, what's a little logical sparring between adversaries? It's all part of the fun, isn't it?

5. Wirecard's Ghost: Has Singapore Learned its Lesson?

The collapse of Wirecard sent shockwaves through the global financial system. It exposed not only the audacity of corporate fraud but also the complicity of trusted advisors — auditors, lawyers, consultants — who turned a blind eye to glaring red flags. The scandal raised urgent questions about professional ethics and regulatory oversight.

Accountability in Corporate Scandals: [6]The Ethical Responsibilities of Lawyers (Auditors, and Consultants)[7][9]

But has anything really changed? The Nuremberg trials etched an enduring principle into the annals of history: "I was just following orders" is no defense. The Wirecard debacle underlined this truth in bold, flashing neon lights: money has a smell, and it's often foul. Yet, as my own legal battles reveal, some in Singapore's legal fraternity seem to have missed the memo.

---

6. *https://medium.com/@slavasolodkiy_67243/wirecards-ghost-has-singapore-learned-its-lesson-69e04f5009be*

7. *https://medium.com/@slavasolodkiy_67243/wirecards-ghost-has-singapore-learned-its-lesson-69e04f5009be*

The R&T & Characterist Conundrum

My opponents from Rajah & Tann, and now Characterist, seem to embody the very ethos Wirecard exposed. Their disregard for the spirit of the law, and their apparent indifference to ethical boundaries raise troubling questions. Have they learned anything from Wirecard? Or are they simply demonstrating that, in some corners of Singapore's legal landscape, the lure of lucrative fees still trumps integrity and the pursuit of justice?

Singapore prides itself on its reputation as a financial hub built on trust and transparency. But the Wirecard scandal, and echoes of it in my own experience, suggest that the city-state may be at a crossroads. Will it strengthen its regulatory framework, ensuring that professional advisors, such as lawyers, are held accountable for their actions? Or will it allow a culture of impunity to fester, where the pursuit of profit overshadows ethical considerations?

The answers to these questions will determine whether Singapore can maintain its standing as a global financial center built on trust and integrity. The ghost of Wirecard looms large, and the world is watching.

Singapore at a Crossroads: The Unanswered Questions

- Has Singapore's legal profession truly internalized the lessons of Wirecard?

- Are there sufficient safeguards in place to prevent a repeat of such scandals?

- Will regulators take decisive action against firms that prioritize their clients' interests over the pursuit of justice?

The collapses of Wirecard and FTX have not only impacted investors and employees but have also raised profound questions about the ethical responsibilities of external professionals — lawyers, auditors, and consultants. Historical precedents like the Nuremberg Trials have long established that professionals cannot evade accountability by claiming they were "just doing their duty."

- **The Imperative of Ethical Responsibility:** The Nuremberg Trials after World War II set a global precedent by declaring that following orders is not a defense for participating in unethical or illegal activities. This principle applies universally, emphasizing that professionals must exercise moral judgment regardless of external pressures.

- **Ignoring the Red Flags:** Wirecard's dramatic fall in 2020 exposed a tangled web of financial deceit that went unnoticed — or was perhaps overlooked — by those tasked with oversight.

- **The Smell of Money:** Despite numerous red flags, Ernst & Young (EY) signed off on Wirecard's accounts for over a decade: EY admitted that they did not independently verify €1 billion in cash held in trust accounts. German authorities fined EY and banned them from taking on new audit clients for two years. Investors filed lawsuits alleging negligence and a breach of auditing standards.

- **Legal Advisors and Ethical Oversight:** Investigations scrutinized whether legal firms enabled fraudulent activities by turning a blind eye to irregularities. Consultants providing compliance services were questioned for their failure to detect or report discrepancies.

FTX's bankruptcy in November 2022 highlighted significant ethical shortcomings in the rapidly evolving cryptocurrency industry too.

- **Lack of Transparency:** FTX employed lesser-known auditing firms, raising concerns about the adequacy of their oversight.

- **Regulatory Scrutiny:** Authorities examined whether auditors met professional standards in a complex, emerging market.

- **Conflict of Interest:** Some legal professionals faced allegations of failing to maintain independent judgment due to close ties with FTX's leadership.

- **Due Diligence Failures:** Consultants were criticized for inadequate risk assessments and not reporting suspicious activities.

- The grand library is on fire! Thousands of manuscripts are burning!
- Have you submitted the 'Conflagration Notification' form?
- There's no time! The entire literary heritage is at stake!
- Sounds like a page-turner! You should probably write a sequel.

The Ethical Breaches, Complicity in Wrongdoing, Negligence and Willful

Blindness

In both Wirecard and FTX, certain professionals appeared to disregard the "smell of money," prioritizing personal or corporate gain over ethical obligations.

- **Ignoring Red Flags:** Professionals overlooked clear signs of wrongdoing.

- **Failure to Act:** There was a lack of timely reporting to authorities or stakeholders.

- **Active Participation:** Some professionals were accused of facilitating fraudulent transactions.

- **Ethical Violations:** Breaches of professional codes of conduct were evident.

The repercussions for ignoring ethical responsibilities have been significant:

- **Revoked Licenses:** Auditors and lawyers faced professional disbarment or suspension.

- **Financial Penalties:** Firms incurred substantial fines and faced costly lawsuits.

- **Reputational Damage:** Trust in these professionals eroded, leading to loss of clients and market credibility.

The Role of Legal Ethics and the Spirit of the Law

Professionals are bound not just by the letter of the law but also by its spirit. Legal ethics demand integrity, impartiality, and a commitment to justice.

- **Duty to Report:** Obligations exist to report illegal activities, even if it means challenging one's employer or client.

- **Independent Judgment:** Professionals must maintain objectivity, avoiding conflicts of interest.

- **Upholding Public Trust:** There is a collective responsibility to ensure the integrity of financial systems and institutions.

The Wirecard and FTX scandals underscore the vital importance of ethical conduct among lawyers, auditors, and consultants. The defense of "just doing my duty" is insufficient when ethical lapses contribute to significant harm. Upholding the spirit of the law and adhering to legal ethics are not optional — they are fundamental responsibilities that safeguard the integrity of the financial system and protect public interest.

Wirecard's Impact on Singapore: Has Singapore Learned Enough?

Wirecard operated in Singapore through its subsidiary, Wirecard Asia Holding Pte Ltd. In 2019, the Singapore police raided Wirecard's offices following reports of accounting irregularities. The Monetary Authority of Singapore (MAS) and the Accounting and Corporate Regulatory Authority (ACRA) began scrutinizing the company's activities, signaling the seriousness of the allegations. Following the scandal, Singapore's regulatory bodies took several steps:

- **Enhanced Oversight:** MAS increased its supervision of payment service providers, emphasizing the need for robust anti-money laundering (AML) and counter-terrorism financing (CTF) measures.

- **Legislative Changes:** The Payment Services Act 2019 was enacted to regulate emerging payment systems and mitigate risks associated with digital transactions.

- **Cross-Border Cooperation:** Singapore strengthened collaboration with international regulators to share information and coordinate responses to financial misconduct.

Lessons Learned and Conclusions Drawn: Legal and Ethical Responsibilities

The Wirecard case highlighted the importance of strong corporate governance:

- **Board Accountability:** Emphasis was placed on the responsibilities of board members to ensure transparency and ethical practices.

- **Audit Rigor:** Calls were made to enhance the independence and effectiveness of both internal and external audits.

But, what's more important — Lawyers and consultants play a crucial role in upholding the integrity of financial systems:

- **Ethical Obligations — Challenges in Legal Ethics:** Legal professionals are reminded of their duty to act in the best interest of justice, not merely in service of their clients.

- **Duty to Report:** There is an expectation for professionals to report suspicious activities to authorities promptly.

While regulatory frameworks have been strengthened, the actions of some industry players raise questions about the extent to which lessons have been internalized. Instances have emerged where legal firms appear to prioritize client interests over ethical considerations:

- **Compliance Gaps:** Some firms have been criticized for insufficient due diligence, potentially enabling unethical practices.

- **Conflicts of Interest:** Close relationships with clients may compromise independent judgment, leading to ethical oversights.

The Role of Firms Like Rajah & Tann and Characterist: Commitment to Ethical Standards

Prominent law firms in Singapore, such as Rajah & Tann and Characterist LLC, have significant influence on industry practices:

- **Leadership Role:** These firms are positioned to lead by example in upholding legal ethics and professional responsibilities.

- **Opportunities for Reflection:** The Wirecard scandal offers a chance for all firms to reassess their practices and ensure alignment with the highest ethical standards.

- **Building Trust:** Upholding ethical practices is essential for maintaining public trust in legal and financial institutions.

- **Accountability:** Firms are encouraged to be transparent about their compliance measures and commitment to ethical conduct.

The Wirecard scandal served as a wake-up call for financial and legal sectors worldwide, including in Singapore. While regulatory bodies have taken significant steps to prevent similar occurrences, the true test lies in the ethical conduct of individual professionals and firms. The actions of industry players suggest that while progress has been made, there is still room for improvement.

Singapore's reputation as a global financial hub depends not only on robust regulations but also on the unwavering commitment of its professionals to uphold the spirit of the law and ethical standards. Continuous vigilance, education, and a culture that prioritizes integrity over convenience are essential to ensure that the hard lessons from Wirecard lead to lasting positive change.

6. On Libel: The Pen Against the Gavel

In the annals of history, truth has often been a beacon guiding societies toward justice, progress, and enlightenment[8][10]. Yet, there have always been those who, cloaked in power and driven by unscrupulous motives, seek to dim this beacon. One of the most insidious tactics employed is the misuse of libel laws—a strategy designed not to protect reputation, but to intimidate, silence, and exhaust those brave enough to unveil inconvenient truths.

Libel laws were conceived as a shield to protect individuals from false and damaging statements. However, in the hands of the powerful, they have been twisted into a sword aimed at the very heart of free expression. Investigative journalists and writers, the stalwarts of truth-telling, often find themselves in the crosshairs of protracted legal battles. These battles are less about vindicating reputation and more about draining resources, instilling fear, and creating a chilling effect on journalism.

Consider the journalist who uncovers corruption, the writer who exposes human rights abuses, or the whistleblower who brings corporate malfeasance to light. Their revelations can catalyze change, ignite public discourse, and hold the mighty accountable. Yet, facing the looming threat of libel lawsuits, many are forced into silence—not because their findings lack merit, but because the personal and financial toll becomes too great to bear.

This misuse of libel laws undermines the very foundations of democracy. A society where truth is suppressed is one where injustice

---

8. https://www.linkedin.com/pulse/libel-pen-against-gavel-vladislav-solodkiy-bdbne/

thrives unchecked. It is imperative to recognize that the suppression of one voice is a loss to all; every silenced story leaves a void where enlightenment could have prevailed.

But amidst this challenge lies an opportunity for resilience and solidarity. History is replete with examples of individuals who, despite overwhelming odds, chose courage over capitulation. Their legacy teaches us that the pursuit of truth is a noble endeavor worth defending.

To the investigative journalists and writers standing at the frontlines: your pen is mightier than any gavel misused to suppress it. Each word you write chips away at walls of deception and builds bridges of understanding. You are not alone in this journey. Support networks, legal advocates, and a global audience hungry for truth stand beside you.

Moreover, it is incumbent upon all of us—readers, citizens, and fellow storytellers—to champion the cause of free expression. We must advocate for legal reforms that prevent the abuse of libel laws, support organizations that defend journalistic integrity, and foster a culture where truth is not just spoken but also protected.

In the face of intimidation, let us find inspiration. Let the attempts to silence be the catalyst that amplifies our collective voice. For every story suppressed, let ten more emerge. Let perseverance be our response to oppression, courage our answer to fear, and truth our weapon against deceit.

The journey toward a just society is neither easy nor without obstacles. But as long as there are those willing to shine a light into the shadows, hope remains. Let us stand united in the conviction that truth cannot be permanently suppressed, and that together, we can ensure it prevails.

How Powerful Figures Use Libel Laws to Silence the Truth

In recent years, a disturbing trend has emerged among the most powerful and, often, the most unscrupulous individuals and corporations: a deliberate and calculated use of legal tactics to suppress the truth. Known as strategic lawsuits against public participation (SLAPP) or simply abuse of libel laws, these lawsuits aim to intimidate, financially drain, and exhaust those who dare to expose corruption, fraud, or criminal activity. Through extensive financial resources, teams of high-powered attorneys, and endless legal maneuvers, these figures exploit the legal system to silence or discredit journalists, writers, and investigators. This practice erodes freedom of speech, hinders the press, and allows serious wrongdoings to continue unchecked, causing far-reaching societal consequences.

Weaponizing Libel Laws to Suppress Investigations

Libel laws are intended to protect individuals from false statements that can harm their reputation, but in the hands of wealthy and influential crooks, they become tools of coercion. When a journalist or investigator uncovers inconvenient truths about these individuals, the response is often swift and severe: a libel lawsuit, replete with accusations of defamation and reputational harm. These lawsuits are not necessarily aimed at winning in court but rather at creating a psychological and financial burden on the defendant.

The typical SLAPP lawsuit tactic is clear: outlast the defendant. The cost of legal representation in complex libel cases can run into hundreds of thousands, if not millions, of dollars—a sum beyond the reach of most individuals, journalists, or small media outlets. While an oligarch or corporation can afford these expenses indefinitely, their targets usually cannot. The aim, then, is not necessarily to win the case but to "wear down" those who expose the truth until they either retract their statements, settle out of court, or become financially ruined.

Hiring "Dream Teams" of Lawyers

One reason this tactic works so well is the financial asymmetry between plaintiffs and defendants. In many cases, the plaintiff hires top legal professionals from major law firms, forming a legal "dream team." These attorneys are highly skilled in using procedural tactics to prolong cases, file endless motions, and appeal any unfavorable rulings. Their clients may be politicians, business magnates, or other influential individuals whose vast resources allow them to hire attorneys whose only job is to make the legal battle as drawn-out and complex as possible.

The media outlet, journalist, or author is often left scrambling to fund their defense, draining their resources in a drawn-out, uphill battle. Many journalists, facing mounting legal bills and the possibility of financial ruin, are forced to retract their stories or settle, even if they possess strong evidence and believe their reporting is accurate. As a result, important stories are silenced, not because they lack merit but because the truth-seekers can't afford to tell them.

Suppressing the Truth with "Chilling Effects"

The ramifications of such legal battles extend far beyond the individuals directly involved. Known as "chilling effects," these lawsuits send a clear message to others in the media: if you dare to investigate or report on us, you risk facing a legal onslaught. This warning creates a climate of fear among journalists, editors, and publishers, who may begin to self-censor rather than risk attracting the ire of those who are both powerful and litigious. Thus, fear of legal repercussions prevents the public from learning about corporate malfeasance, political corruption, and criminal enterprise, allowing wrongdoers to operate with impunity.

Even well-established publications are sometimes forced to withhold stories or avoid reporting on certain figures to mitigate potential legal exposure. Authors often face pushback from publishers who fear the financial and reputational consequences of a libel lawsuit. In some cases, books are "preemptively" censored, with publishers removing entire sections or even scrapping planned releases to avoid legal entanglements.

The Social Cost: A Distorted Public Narrative

The impact of such tactics goes far beyond individual cases. When the truth is suppressed, society at large suffers, as people are left in the dark about critical issues. In a democracy, an informed public is essential for holding power to account, but these lawsuits distort the information landscape, creating a narrative that favors those with wealth and influence over those who tell the truth. Without access to accurate, investigative journalism, the public is deprived of essential information needed to make informed decisions about everything from voting to social policy.

Abuse: Intimidation and Financial Burden

There are numerous cases where public figures or corporations have successfully suppressed negative information by abusing libel laws. For example, journalists and authors who have written about high-profile businessmen involved in questionable financial practices frequently find themselves entangled in lawsuits. In some cases, they are sued in jurisdictions that are known for "libel tourism," where the plaintiff cherry-picks a location with laws favorable to their case, making it even more difficult for the defendant to mount an effective defense.

One particularly insidious example is how these individuals strategically use legal action to block book publications. A writer may spend years researching and writing a book, only to have it pulled from shelves or heavily edited after threats of legal action. Investigative journalists, who often spend years working on explosive stories, face similar threats. Their only options may be to retract or heavily modify the reporting, even if it's based on rigorous fact-checking and solid sources.

I am very grateful to Rebecca Ratcliffe[9][11] from The Guardian[10] for sharing her article about Kokila Annamalai[11] – and huge thanks to Jane Croft[12] from FT too:

---

9. https://www.linkedin.com/posts/vsolodkiy_i-am-very-grateful-to-rebecca-ratcliffe-activity-

    7260359820854050816-okx5/

10. https://www.linkedin.com/company/theguardian/

11. https://www.linkedin.com/in/kokila-annamalai-91150218/

her article on defamation law reforms to prevent abuses by wealthy plaintiffs is highly relevant to my situation, as it describes a similar dynamic, how influential and wealthy individuals use lawsuits to suppress criticism and restrict free speech. Recommended reading: **Putin's People** - by Catherine Belton[13]; **Kleptopia** - by Tom Burgis[14]; **Money Men** - by Dan McCrum[15]; PATRIOT[16] - by Alexei Navalny.

Alexei Navalny's experiences provide a compelling example of how powerful individuals and governments misuse libel laws and other legal mechanisms to suppress the truth and silence critics

Navalny, a Russian opposition leader and anti-corruption activist, has been a vocal critic of corruption within the Russian government and among influential oligarchs. His efforts to expose wrongdoing have often been met with legal retaliation designed to intimidate and silence him.

Defamation Lawsuits and Legal Pressure: Legal System as a Tool for Suppression

Navalny has faced numerous defamation lawsuits filed by powerful figures whom he has accused of corrupt practices. These lawsuits often result in substantial fines and are part of a broader strategy to drain his resources and hinder his investigative work. For example:

- **Yevgeny Prigozhin Lawsuit:** In 2019, a court ordered Navalny and his Anti-Corruption Foundation (FBK) to pay significant damages to a company linked to Yevgeny

---

12. https://www.linkedin.com/in/jane-croft-7babb1290/

13. https://www.linkedin.com/in/catherine-belton-817260a/

14. https://www.linkedin.com/in/tom-burgis-35671316/

15. https://www.linkedin.com/in/dan-mccrum-b985a47/

16. https://amzn.to/3UAvUoN

Prigozhin, a businessman with close ties to the Kremlin. The lawsuit was over a video alleging corruption in a school meals contract, and the hefty fine threatened the financial viability of Navalny's organization.

- **Alisher Usmanov Case:** In 2017, billionaire Alisher Usmanov sued Navalny for defamation after Navalny released a report alleging corrupt dealings between Usmanov and then-Prime Minister Dmitry Medvedev. The court ruled in favor of Usmanov, ordering Navalny to remove the investigative materials from his websites.

These legal actions serve not necessarily to clear the plaintiffs' names but to burden Navalny with legal and financial obstacles.

The lawsuits consume time, resources, and divert attention away from his anti-corruption efforts.

Beyond defamation lawsuits, the Russian government has employed various legal tactics to suppress Navalny's activities:

- **Criminal Charges:** Navalny has been prosecuted on multiple occasions on charges that many international observers and human rights organizations consider politically motivated. These prosecutions have resulted in house arrests, jail time, and restrictions on his political activities.

- **Designation of Extremism:** In June 2021, Russian courts labeled Navalny's organizations as "extremist," effectively banning them and exposing staff and supporters to criminal prosecution. This designation prevents his organizations from operating legally and further silences dissenting voices.

- **Financial Investigations:** Authorities have conducted financial probes into Navalny's organizations, accusing them of money laundering and other financial crimes. These investigations strain the organizations' operations and deter donors and supporters due to fear of legal repercussions.

Impact on Free Speech and Society: Global Recognition and Response

The actions against Navalny exemplify how libel laws and the legal system can be manipulated by those in power to suppress investigative journalism and dissent:

- **Chilling Effect:** The aggressive use of defamation lawsuits and legal charges creates a chilling effect on other journalists, activists, and citizens who might expose corruption or criticize the government, fearing similar retaliation.

- **Suppression of Information:** By silencing Navalny and dismantling his organizations, the government restricts public access to information about corruption and abuses of power, undermining transparency and accountability.

- **Erosion of Democratic Principles:** The misuse of legal mechanisms to target critics erodes the rule of law and democratic institutions, as laws intended to protect citizens are repurposed to suppress them.

Navalny's situation has drawn international attention,

highlighting the broader issue of how authoritarian regimes and powerful individuals use libel laws to stifle free speech:

- **International Condemnation:** Governments, international organizations, and human rights groups have condemned the legal actions against Navalny, calling for his release and the protection of fundamental freedoms.

- **Inspiration for Anti-Corruption Efforts:** Despite the repression, Navalny's work has inspired others worldwide to continue the fight against corruption and advocate for democratic reforms.

Alexei Navalny's experiences vividly illustrate how libel laws and the legal system can be weaponized by powerful figures to intimidate, silence, and exhaust those who seek to expose the truth.

His case underscores the critical need for legal safeguards that protect freedom of speech and ensure that laws serve justice rather than suppress it. By understanding and addressing these abuses, society can work towards preserving the essential democratic values of transparency, accountability, and the free exchange of ideas.

Navalny's experiences underscore how powerful individuals can exploit legal systems to intimidate and suppress those who challenge them. Though Russia's approach involves more extreme tactics, including criminal charges and overt censorship, the core principle is the same as in countries where libel laws are misused. In both cases, the aim is to silence dissent and control narratives by wielding legal power against individuals without the resources to fight back on equal footing.

Navalny's case also demonstrates the resilience required to withstand these tactics.

By making his findings as public as possible and rallying public support, Navalny has managed to continue his work despite overwhelming odds. His experience serves as a potent reminder that protecting investigative journalism and activism from legal abuse is essential to upholding transparency, accountability, and democracy.

Part 3: Suing the System: A Self-Litigant's Journey with AI and the Fight for a Fairer Courtroom

AI vs. Goliath: *Hercules in the Courtroom*

7. Self-Litigant Costs Reimbursement

The argument that compensating a self-litigant's time is unfair because they are not professional lawyers is not only illogical but also discriminatory[1][12]. It harkens back to a time when access to justice was the privilege of the elite, a stark contrast to the modern ideals of equality and fairness. Should a self-litigant, forced into that position by their opponent's machinations, be penalized for lacking a title? Is their time, their knowledge, their relentless fight for justice any less valuable?

The fact that this discrimination can be based on race, nationality, gender, or orientation adds another layer of injustice. It creates a system where certain individuals are inherently disadvantaged, their voices stifled, their rights denied.

Singaporean courts, known for their fairness and efficiency, must address this glaring inequity. Drawing inspiration from international cases like Cachia v Hanes and Oshlack v Richmond River Council in Australia, where the courts recognized the right to compensation for self-litigants and the importance of considering exceptional circumstances, Singapore can pave the way for a more just system.

It is time for Singapore to champion the cause of the self-litigant, to acknowledge the value of their time and effort. It is time to reject the discriminatory notion that only those with the title of a lawyer deserve compensation for their work. It is time for a system that truly ensures equality before the law, regardless of wealth or professional designation. Only then can justice be said to be served.

---

1. https://www.facebook.com/vladislavsolodkiy/posts/pfbid02qC3SNuLQQGSnkdmaA45kaB5bnDBaLwyJc1z9DEdgHjUp14dv2T75FV3yykCS3SZWl

8. The Cynicism of It All: The Domino Effect of Impunity

If such behavior is allowed to persist unchecked, what message does it send to other aspiring corporate puppeteers[1][13]? Will Singapore become a haven for those seeking to **exploit loopholes and manipulate the legal system** for their own gain? Will the pursuit of justice become a Sisyphean task, reserved only for those with the deepest pockets and the strongest resolve?

Let's not forget the grand HC spectacle, a legal drama worthy of Shakespeare himself. It's a tale of convoluted claims and counterclaims, a labyrinth of procedural maneuvers designed to confuse and confound.

The irony is palpable. The very individuals who claim to be champions of corporate governance and minority shareholder rights are the ones actively undermining those principles. They're playing a game of legal chess, where the pieces are not pawns and knights, but the livelihoods and reputations of those who dare to question their authority.

---

1. https://www.linkedin.com/posts/vsolodkiy_the-predictability-of-rts-tactics-the-activity-7245433812044718081-LoGx/?utm_source=share&utm_medium=member_desktop

9. Confidentiality Clauses and Other Fairy Tales: An Open Letter

An Ironic Journey Through Legal Labyrinths

Their insistence on confidentiality is not merely inconvenient; it's downright alarming. It's as if they're saying, "We'll pay you to look the other way, to pretend that this never happened, to let us continue our shadowy dealings undisturbed." But sunlight, as they say, is the best disinfectant, and I, for one, refuse to be complicit in their darkness.

If they are so confident in their righteousness, if their actions are above reproach, then why this aversion to public scrutiny? Why the desperate need to bury the truth beneath layers of legal jargon and non-disclosure agreements? It seems that the prospect of their actions being exposed to the harsh light of day is far more terrifying to them than any potential financial loss.

An Open Letter to the Persistent Pursuers

Dear Advocates of Absolute Confidentiality, Rajah & Tann (and Characterist now too), it seems there's been a misunderstanding — or perhaps a series of them. Repetition, while a favored tactic in advertising, doesn't magically transform an untenable proposition into an acceptable one. Insisting on the same point ad infinitum without addressing the counterarguments is, at best, an exercise in futility.

Let me be unequivocally clear: I'm open to negotiations on many fronts, but confidentiality isn't one of them. Your unwavering commitment to this demand, despite numerous rejections, has compelled me to address the matter publicly. Consider this the result of your own perseverance.

We are all adults here — or so I've been led to believe. It's high time we take responsibility for our actions and cease with the lamentations. The tides are turning, and while I offered an olive branch in the past, it was met with indifference. Now, as the scales begin to tip, it's curious to see a renewed interest in settlement — but only on terms that serve to obscure rather than resolve.

Part 4: The Emotional and Financial Toll Beyond the Letter: AI and the Ethical Revolution in Law

No Lawyer, No Problem! Rewriting the Rules: Self-Litigation and the Rise of AI Justice

10. Filed for Personal Bankruptcy & Gave Up: When 'Winning' Means Losing Everything

The Unseen Struggle: When the Legal System Becomes a Weapon

It's been a year since my life took an unexpected and devastating turn[1][14]. In the world of startups and venture capital, I was considered a success story. But behind the facade of achievement, a silent battle raged that would ultimately strip me of everything I had worked for.

Forced into Bankruptcy: When 'Winning' Costs Everything

It began with a seemingly promising investment in Arival Pte Ltd. However, what started as a partnership soon devolved into a nightmare. The majority shareholders and directors, driven by motives I still struggle to comprehend, launched a campaign of legal warfare against me.

Lawsuit after lawsuit piled up, each one a carefully calculated attack designed to drain my finances, consume my time, and break my spirit. I was dragged through a labyrinth of legal procedures, forced to navigate a complex system without the resources to afford proper representation.

Bankrupted by Justice: How 'Victory' Led to My Downfall

Imagine this: you're a single individual facing off against a team of highly paid lawyers from top-tier firms. Your days are consumed with

---

1. https://medium.com/@slavasolodkiy_67243/filed-for-personal-bankruptcy-gave-up-when-winning-means-losing-everything-eaf5e5ad1bbc

responding to motions, filing counterclaims, and desperately trying to keep your head above water. The stress is relentless, impacting your health, your relationships, and your very sense of self.

This isn't a story about bad investments or poor financial decisions. It's about the abuse of power, the weaponization of the legal system, and the devastating consequences of corporate bullying. It's about the unseen struggles that can lie hidden beneath a veneer of success.

When 'Winning' Means Losing It All: My Battle with Injustice

I've been forced to file for personal bankruptcy in three countries — Singapore, the UK, and the US[2]. My career, built over two decades, hangs in the balance. My reputation, once a source of pride, is now tarnished by the very people who owe me a debt of gratitude.

But even in the face of such adversity, I refuse to be silenced. I will continue to fight for justice, not just for myself, but for anyone who has been victimized by those who exploit the legal system for their own gain.

The High Price of 'Victory': Filing for Bankruptcy Against All Odds

This is a story of resilience, of the human spirit's ability to endure even in the darkest of times. It's a call for awareness, for a system that protects the vulnerable and holds the powerful accountable. It's a reminder that even when it seems like all is lost, the fight for justice is always worth fighting.

---

2. https://www.linkedin.com/posts/vsolodkiy_the-paradox-of-self-representation-advancing-activity-7263150185919176704-06Fe/?utm_source=share&utm_medium=member_desktop

11. How Powerful Crooks Weaponize the Law to Silence Critics

In an ideal world, justice prevails, and those who expose wrongdoing are lauded as heroes. However, reality often presents a starkly different picture[1][15]. The biggest, most ruthless, and cynical crooks, those with vast resources and influence, have increasingly turned to a chilling tactic: weaponizing the legal system to silence those who dare to speak truth to power.

These individuals, often shielded by a veneer of respectability, understand that legal battles are costly, time-consuming, and emotionally draining. By wielding lawsuits like blunt instruments, they aim to intimidate, exhaust, and ultimately bankrupt their critics. The accusation of libel, frequently leveled against journalists, authors, and investigators, becomes a powerful tool in their arsenal.

The strategy is simple yet devastatingly effective. These powerful individuals assemble teams of high-priced lawyers, experts in exploiting legal loopholes and maneuvering through the complexities of defamation law. They bury their opponents in paperwork, depositions, and court appearances, stretching out the process for months, even years. The financial burden alone can be crippling, forcing many to abandon their pursuit of justice simply to survive.

Even when these lawsuits lack merit, they serve their purpose. The threat of legal action hangs like a sword of Damocles, creating a chilling effect on free speech. Journalists and publishers become hesitant to expose wrongdoing, fearing the potential repercussions. Sources dry up, investigations stall, and the truth remains hidden.

---

1. https://medium.com/@slavasolodkiy_67243/how-powerful-crooks-weaponize-the-law-to-silence-critics-a7b6966d5969

This abuse of the legal system not only harms those directly targeted but also undermines the very foundation of a democratic society. The free flow of information, the ability to hold the powerful accountable, is essential for a healthy democracy. When those in power can manipulate the law to shield themselves from scrutiny, corruption flourishes, and trust in institutions erodes.

While the situation may seem bleak, there is hope. Organizations dedicated to defending free speech and supporting investigative journalism are fighting back, providing legal assistance and raising awareness about this insidious tactic. Ultimately, it is the responsibility of all citizens to demand a system where truth prevails over intimidation and where justice is accessible to all, not just the wealthy and powerful.

ENRC vs. Financial Times and Tom Burgis: A Victory for Free Speech

Kleptopia[2]: How Dirty Money is Conquering the World — by Tom Burgis

The case of Tom Burgis and the Financial Times (FT) against Eurasian Natural Resources Corporation (ENRC) is a potent example of the so-called "libel chill." Burgis, an investigative journalist, authored Kleptopia: How Dirty Money is Conquering the World, in which he detailed allegations of corruption and money laundering against ENRC. ENRC argued that Burgis had defamed the corporation, asserting that parts of his book implied the company had engaged in criminal activities. This lawsuit was viewed as part of a broader strategy to suppress investigative journalism around the dealings of large corporations, especially those operating in regions with limited regulatory oversight.

---
2. *https://amzn.to/4bLfKDl*

The High Court, however, dismissed ENRC's claim, ruling in favor of Burgis and the FT. This outcome marked a significant win for investigative journalism, affirming that allegations of misconduct, when based on credible research and sources, cannot be easily suppressed through libel lawsuits. Despite this victory, the case highlighted the immense legal costs and psychological strain that journalists face when taking on multinational corporations backed by legal "dream teams."

Catherine Belton and Putin's People: A Relentless Legal Assault

Putin's People[3]: The Story of Russia's History and Politics — by Catherine Belton

Catherine Belton's Putin's People became an international bestseller for its in-depth exploration of the Russian oligarchs and their ties to Vladimir Putin. However, the book soon attracted a barrage of lawsuits from some of the world's wealthiest individuals, including Russian oligarch Roman Abramovich and state energy company Rosneft. Abramovich claimed the book defamed him by citing claims from former Kremlin insider Sergei Pugachev, who alleged Abramovich had acted as a personal financier for Putin. Rosneft argued that Belton's descriptions of their operations unfairly painted them as Kremlin-controlled tools.

HarperCollins, the book's publisher, and Belton were forced into a grueling legal process. The financial and emotional toll on both author and publisher was enormous. Despite ultimately settling with Abramovich and others, which involved amending certain parts of the book, Belton's case underscores how deep-pocketed plaintiffs can disrupt and control narratives around their activities through libel lawsuits.

---

3. https://amzn.to/40xdAB0

Belton's experience shines a light on the ways legal threats are weaponized to prevent critical voices from reaching a wider audience, forcing journalists and publishers to make difficult compromises to avoid potentially ruinous financial repercussions. Nonetheless, the fact that Belton and HarperCollins could bring Putin's People to the public shows the resilience and tenacity required in modern investigative journalism, especially when confronting the powerful.

Dan McCrum and the Wirecard Scandal: Surveillance, Smear Campaigns, and Lawsuits

Money Men[4]: A Hot Startup, A Billion Dollar Fraud, A Fight for the Truth — by Dan McCrum

Dan McCrum's investigation into Wirecard stands as one of the most harrowing examples of how far corporations will go to silence journalists. McCrum, a Financial Times reporter, spent six years investigating Wirecard, a German payments processor lauded for its growth and innovation. Wirecard's numbers, however, didn't add up, and McCrum's reporting revealed signs of deep-seated fraud. But rather than owning up to these issues, Wirecard launched an aggressive counter-campaign.

Wirecard not only sued McCrum and the FT but also launched a coordinated smear campaign against him and his wife, which included harassment and surveillance. Wirecard worked with private investigators and PR agencies to portray McCrum as untrustworthy and even suggested that he was financially motivated to damage the company. German regulators and banks, perhaps embarrassed by their failure to identify the fraud sooner, added to the pressure on McCrum, investigating FT's reporting methods instead of the company's business practices.

---

4. https://amzn.to/3YxUfNt

Despite these attacks, McCrum persisted, and his reporting ultimately contributed to exposing one of the largest corporate frauds in modern German history. The scandal led to Wirecard's collapse and the arrest of several executives. McCrum's story highlights the exceptional challenges faced by journalists who dare to question corporate narratives and bring hidden truths to light. The Wirecard case emphasizes the complex, multi-layered attacks that corporations can mount — not just in court, but also through PR campaigns, surveillance, and even influencing regulators.

The Common Thread: Suppression of the Truth through Legal and Financial Leverage

These cases underscore a common theme: powerful figures leveraging vast resources to suppress journalism. Each of these corporations and individuals used a variety of tools, from libel lawsuits to public smear campaigns, to obstruct the publication of inconvenient truths. Such tactics reveal the lengths to which those with financial and legal power will go to keep their reputations intact, even if it means undermining freedom of speech.

The chilling effect on journalism is profound. Even when cases are ultimately dismissed, the process serves as a warning to others: that attempting to investigate the powerful can lead to years of court battles, surveillance, and financial hardship. Many media outlets, especially smaller ones, may think twice before publishing investigative pieces on powerful individuals or companies due to the potentially devastating consequences.

Toward a Solution: Anti-SLAPP Legislation

To combat these issues, there is a growing call for anti-SLAPP (Strategic Lawsuit Against Public Participation) legislation, which would allow judges to dismiss frivolous lawsuits aimed at silencing criticism. Several countries have already implemented such laws, but they are far from universal. Stronger anti-SLAPP laws, alongside increased legal support for journalists, would help level the playing field and protect reporters and publishers from being bankrupted by abusive litigation.

Organizations like the Committee to Protect Journalists, Reporters Without Borders, and various press freedom groups are also instrumental in supporting journalists facing legal threats. However, the financial burden and emotional toll of these battles remain high, highlighting the need for greater solidarity and support within the media industry to defend the right to report the truth.

Countering this abuse requires a multi-faceted approach. First, legal reforms to discourage frivolous or strategically intimidating libel lawsuits are essential. Some jurisdictions have implemented anti-SLAPP laws, which allow defendants to have meritless cases dismissed quickly and sometimes reclaim legal fees. Expanding and strengthening these laws globally could provide greater protection for journalists and truth-tellers.

Second, there is a growing need to provide financial and legal support for investigative journalism. Organizations like the Committee to Protect Journalists (CPJ) and the Reporters Committee for Freedom of the Press offer financial and legal aid to journalists under threat. However, more resources are needed to level the playing field and ensure that journalists, writers, and small media outlets are not forced into silence due to a lack of resources.

The cases of Tom Burgis, Catherine Belton, and Dan McCrum illustrate how the powerful use legal maneuvers to stifle investigative journalism. While these journalists ultimately prevailed, their victories came at great cost and underscore the urgent need for legal reforms and support mechanisms to protect those who dare to expose corruption, fraud, and abuse of power.

Until such reforms are widespread, the world will continue to see cases where those with money and influence can suppress stories, leaving citizens uninformed and allowing wrongdoing to persist unchecked. To protect truth-telling, a global commitment to defending journalistic freedom and fighting legal intimidation is essential. In an era where truth is increasingly under attack, the courage of these journalists reminds us of the high stakes involved in the battle for transparency and accountability.

The rise of libel lawsuits by powerful individuals and corporations to intimidate journalists represents a severe threat to free speech and the dissemination of truth. When used by the most ruthless and cynical figures, libel laws have become tools of oppression, allowing those with wealth and influence to escape accountability and suppress critical information. Without protections against such abuses, society risks losing one of its most valuable resources: the freedom to know and seek the truth.

As history shows, unchecked power leads to corruption. If we are to defend democracy, justice, and truth, it is crucial to counter the misuse of libel laws by the rich and powerful. Only then can we ensure that our legal systems serve not as shields for the unscrupulous but as tools for upholding justice and transparency.

Navalny's Counter to Libel-like Practices: Transparency and Publicity

PATRIOT[5]: memoir and secret prison diaries by the fearless Russian opposition leader — by Alexei Navalny

Alexei Navalny, the prominent Russian opposition leader and anti-corruption activist, is a prime example of how powerful individuals in Russia use libel lawsuits to silence and suppress critics. Here's how Navalny's case connects to the "libel" practice:

- **Systematic Targeting:** Navalny has been repeatedly targeted with libel lawsuits by individuals close to the Kremlin or those with vested interests in maintaining the

---

5. *https://amzn.to/3UAvUoN*

status quo. These lawsuits often follow his investigations exposing corruption among high-ranking officials.

- **Frivolous Claims:** Many of the lawsuits filed against Navalny appear to be based on flimsy or fabricated accusations. The intent seems less about winning the case and more about draining his resources, damaging his reputation, and distracting him from his anti-corruption work.

- **Financial Burden:** The legal costs associated with defending himself against multiple lawsuits have been substantial, putting a strain on Navalny's organization and potentially hindering its ability to operate effectively.

- **Chilling Effect:** The constant threat of legal action creates a hostile environment for investigative journalism and dissent in Russia. It discourages others from speaking out against corruption or challenging those in power.

- **International Condemnation:** The international community has widely condemned the use of libel laws against Navalny, recognizing them as a form of political persecution.

Navalny's case highlights the dangers faced by those who dare to challenge powerful individuals and expose corruption. It underscores the urgent need for greater protection of free speech and the fight against the misuse of legal systems for political purposes.

There is a significant connection between Alexei Navalny's experiences and the broader issue of how powerful individuals and corporations weaponize libel lawsuits and other forms of legal intimidation to silence critics and investigative journalists. Navalny's work as an anti-corruption activist and political opponent of powerful Russian elites has exposed him to a variety of tactics aimed at silencing and discrediting him. While his experience extends beyond typical libel suits, it vividly illustrates the lengths to which influential figures will go to prevent damaging information from reaching the public.

Weaponized Lawsuits to Deter Investigations: Blocking Information Through Legal Intimidation

Navalny's Anti-Corruption Foundation (FBK) has exposed corruption within the Russian government, particularly focusing on high-ranking officials and oligarchs close to Vladimir Putin. In response, Russian authorities and influential business figures have launched a series of lawsuits against Navalny and FBK. These lawsuits, while not always framed as libel, function similarly: they aim to drain resources, deter further investigation, and intimidate those involved.

For instance, after Navalny published investigations linking various Russian oligarchs to corrupt practices, several of these individuals filed legal claims against him and his organization, accusing him of slander and defamation. This tactic mirrors libel lawsuits used by corporations and individuals in other countries to silence journalists, with the lawsuits often seeking damages large enough to financially cripple the target.

In countries with strong free press protections, libel laws are sometimes misused to intimidate journalists and suppress uncomfortable truths. In Russia, however, legal systems are often directly controlled or influenced by powerful elites, making it even easier to shut down dissent. Navalny's investigative videos and online publications have faced aggressive censorship. Lawsuits against him are accompanied by state-imposed shutdowns of his online platforms, fines, and even attempts to ban his content outright under vague legal pretexts, such as "extremism" or "disinformation."

For instance, following his investigation into "Putin's Palace" (a luxury estate allegedly constructed for the Russian president through illicit funds), Navalny faced an escalation of both legal charges and attempts to block the information. Russian authorities removed his content from mainstream platforms, attempting to erase it from public view, much like the way libel suits seek to retract or suppress information through the courts.

Financial and Psychological Drain Through Lawsuits and Legal Pressure

Navalny, like many investigative journalists, has faced enormous financial burdens due to constant legal battles. His organization and its employees have been fined repeatedly, leading to mounting legal expenses and financial strain. In many cases, these fines are intended to deter not just Navalny but anyone connected to him from pursuing further investigations.

In the context of libel practices globally, this mirrors SLAPP lawsuits (strategic lawsuits against public participation), which rely on financial drain and intimidation as primary tactics. Whether through libel laws or more extreme measures, the goal remains the same: to financially exhaust the individual or organization, forcing them to choose between financial ruin and silence.

When Navalny releases new findings, he often faces a concerted effort by the Russian state and its allies to discredit him personally. In the case of the "Putin's Palace" investigation, Russian state media ran counter-narratives, portraying him as a foreign agent, a liar, or even accusing him of personal misconduct. This is a tactic frequently employed by powerful individuals in libel cases: they not only sue for defamation but also seek to discredit the journalist or investigator's reputation by casting doubt on their motives, ethics, or character.

Similarly, powerful individuals facing defamation claims often respond with PR campaigns, painting themselves as victims of "biased" or "unfair" media. In Navalny's case, however, the counter-narrative is often propagated on a national scale, utilizing state resources to shape public opinion against him.

Navalny has ingeniously countered these libel-like practices by leveraging public transparency. Instead of quietly settling claims or retracting statements under pressure, he publishes his findings openly, making it difficult for those he investigates to silence him without attracting public scrutiny. By embracing transparency, Navalny has managed to turn accusations against him into public discussions on corruption, mobilizing support and circumventing some of the suppression tactics used against him.

This method — using public interest as a form of protection — is a common strategy among journalists facing libel lawsuits. By raising awareness, journalists and activists hope to generate enough public support to protect themselves and counter legal intimidation.

12. My Personal Bankruptcy in the UK, US, and Singapore

In a world saturated with social media portrayals of success and happiness, it's easy to forget that everyone has their own silent battles. Today, I want to share my story[1][16], not for sympathy, but to shed light on a harsh reality that anyone could face. I've spent the last two decades building a career in the financial sector, achieving milestones and accolades along the way. Yet, here I am, on the verge of personal bankruptcy in three countries – Singapore, the UK, and the US.

How did this happen? It's simple: I became a target. The majority shareholders and directors of Arival Pte Ltd, a company I invested in, have waged a relentless legal war against me. Their tactic? Endless lawsuits, frivolous claims, and procedural delays, all designed to exhaust my resources and break my spirit.

Imagine this: you're drowning in legal paperwork, forced to represent yourself because your supposed wealth is tied up in shares and unfulfilled debt obligations. Your health deteriorates, your career crumbles, and your reputation is dragged through the mud.

This isn't a tale of financial mismanagement or personal irresponsibility. It's a stark reminder that the legal system, designed to uphold justice, can be weaponized for personal gain. It's about the crushing weight of endless litigation, the emotional toll of battling giants, and the injustice of having your hard-earned success ripped away.

I'm sharing my story not to elicit pity, but to spark a conversation. It's time to question a system that allows such abuse, to demand

---

1. https://www.facebook.com/vladislavsolodkiy/posts/

pfbid06vVi5saqdXeFRVN9o19H2JLkovD1csRTuovzMPb8miQ3uv39Ur8fd6Dna3Jo6FY7l accountability from those who exploit it, and to stand up for those who find themselves trapped in its gears.

This isn't just about me; it's about the potential for anyone to become ensnared in a similar web. It's about the need for fairness, transparency, and a legal system that prioritizes justice over attrition. I may be down, but I'm not out. I'll rebuild, I'll repay, and I'll emerge stronger. But more importantly, I'll fight for a world where the legal system is a shield, not a sword.

https://l.Nansen.id/change.org[2]

---

2. https://l.nansen.id/change.org

Part 5: Justice for All: Ethics, AI, and the Self-Litigant Revolution

*The **Algorithm of Justice**: How **AI** is Disrupting the Legal Landscape and Empowering the People*

A lawyer falls into a deep pit.
A traveler peers over the edge. "Need a hand?"
The lawyer muses, "Before you help, can we discuss whether assistance is an objective good or merely a social contract?"
"Perhaps I'll come back later," the traveler says, walking away.

13. The Predictability of R&T's Tactics: The Theater of Arival's Absurd

Ah, the dance of justice continues, and as predicted[1][17], our esteemed opponents, Javonsher (Rashidovich) Abdullaev[2] and Shukrullo (Shukur) Israilov[3] (and Sharof Sharipov[4] too), the paragons of corporate virtue and transparency, have once again graced me with R&T lawyers[5] and their predictable waltz of delay and obfuscation. Three (Four?) times they have extended their olive branch, their hands outstretched not with a gesture of reconciliation, but with a contract demanding silence. A contract that whispers, "Take the money and forget the truth, lest you upset the delicate balance of our carefully constructed narrative."

The Mysterious Case of the Persistent Confidentiality Clause

Gather 'round, dear readers, for a tale as old as time — or at least as old as the ink on the latest legal documents I've received. It appears that some things in life are inevitable, and the insistent push for confidentiality clauses by certain parties in legal settlements. Who knew?

Yes, indeed, the defendants — let's call them "J and S" to preserve a semblance of decorum — major shareholders and directors of a certain company we'll refer to as "A Ltd" to keep things delightfully vague,

---

1. https://medium.com/@slavasolodkiy_67243/the-predictability-of-r-ts-tactics-the-theater-of-the-arival-s-absurd-45f0690d8376
2. https://ae.linkedin.com/in/javonsher
3. https://offshoreleaks.icij.org/nodes/56061528
4. https://uk.linkedin.com/in/sharof
5. https://en.wikipedia.org/wiki/Rajah_%26_Tann

have already approached me not once, not twice, but three-four times with offers for a "settlement." Each offer, however, comes with a catch as predictable as a plot twist in a daytime soap: the ever-present, all-encompassing demand for confidentiality.

Now, I won't bore you with the minutiae of their proposals (and certainly not divulge any confidential terms — heaven forbid!). But let's just say that their fixation on keeping things hush-hush has become the elephant in the courtroom.

Fear and Loathing in Legal Negotiations

Allow me to draw your attention to this recurring detail — not only does it not suit me, but it also raises a few eyebrows:

First, I lack the vast resources that the defendants seemingly have at their disposal. Publicity has historically been one of my trusty tools — a sort of legal Swiss Army knife, if you will. Silence might be golden for some, but for me, it's merely gilded cage bars.

Second, if the defendants are entirely above board and I'm destined to lose, what, pray tell, are they so afraid of? I'm perfectly willing to voice my thoughts openly and accept the consequences. It's fascinating how those accustomed to navigating murky waters tend to recoil at the first sign of daylight.

Third, consider the fascinating world of crime statistics: many repeat offenses occur because the initial misdeed wasn't adequately addressed. Singapore, renowned for its stringent adherence to law and order, serves as a beacon in this regard. What happens to our fair society when certain players can not only sidestep repercussions but also demand absolute secrecy about their actions? It's a slippery slope paved with good intentions — or perhaps not-so-good ones.

The Art of Offering Crumbs

In reality, what's being presented to me is the chance to win a few skirmishes while effectively conceding the war. The defendants attempt to slice and dice my claims into isolated incidents, each wrapped neatly in a confidentiality ribbon. It's the gift that keeps on giving — except the gift is an empty box.

Their 'settlement' offers are, shall we say, less than adequate. They seem to operate under the assumption that I've been worn down to the point where any token gesture will suffice to buy my silence. It's a classic strategy: divide, conquer, and hope the opposition runs out of steam (or funds) before the main event.

The Perils of Silence

But here's the rub: accepting such terms doesn't just impact me. It sets a precedent, a beacon to others who might think that dubious practices can be swept under the rug with a well-placed confidentiality clause. Today it's me; tomorrow, it's any number of minority shareholders who find themselves outmaneuvered not by superior arguments but by deeper pockets.

Often, remaining silent in the face of wrongdoing isn't just a personal compromise — it's a tacit endorsement of the behavior. Complicity through silence is a luxury I can't afford, and neither can the broader community that values transparency and fairness.

A Public Stand

Given this continuous and intensifying pressure, I've concluded that the only viable defense is to bring these matters into the open. Sunlight is, after all, the best disinfectant. Without delving into the confidential details (because that would be impolite, wouldn't it?), I hereby firmly and irrevocably refuse to grant the defendants the cloak of confidentiality they've so ardently sought.

This isn't just about me. It's about all the others who might find themselves in similar predicaments — individuals who may lack the means or the platform to voice their concerns. It's about maintaining a business environment where fairness isn't just an ideal but a practiced reality.

The Inevitable Outcome

To paraphrase a well-worn adage, you can't have your cake and eat it too — especially if you're trying to hide the cake under a blanket of secrecy. The information about the outcomes of these proceedings isn't a bargaining chip to be sequestered away for convenience. It is, and will remain, part of the broader narrative that underscores a pattern of behavior.

In closing, it's worth noting that playing fair isn't just about adhering to the letter of the law but embracing its spirit. Winning isn't everything, but how one plays the game speaks volumes. Perhaps it's time to revisit the rulebook — not to find loopholes, but to understand the value of integrity.

This journey has been as enlightening as it has been challenging. While the path of least resistance often tempts with its simplicity, it's rarely the route that leads to meaningful change. By choosing transparency over silence, I aim not just to address my own grievances but to contribute to a culture where accountability isn't optional.

To those who find themselves facing similar crossroads, remember: the demand for secrecy often speaks louder than any confession. Stand firm, question incessantly, and never underestimate the power of bringing things into the light.

The Final Act of an Unconventional Odyssey

As we draw the curtains on this saga of corporate intrigue, legal gymnastics, and the relentless pursuit of transparency, it's only fitting to reflect on the journey from its tumultuous beginnings to its ironic climax.

It all started with a simple premise: a minority shareholder and occasional creditor (that's me) standing up against the tides of corporate conformity. The stage was set with directors and majority shareholders wielding their influence like seasoned conductors, orchestrating a symphony designed to drown out dissenting voices. Their instruments of choice? [Forbidden to mention] proceedings, withheld debts, and the ever-persistent confidentiality clause — a trifecta of tactics aimed at wearing down the opposition.

But let's not forget the ensemble cast. Enter the legal maestros from esteemed firms, whose roles seemed to blur the lines between defense and, well, something less noble. Their strategies often felt like a masterclass in evasion, focusing on form over substance, and details over the bigger picture. It's as if they believed that by constructing an elaborate maze of procedural hurdles, the essence of the matter might conveniently get lost within.

Throughout this odyssey, I endeavored not to mirror their vagueness but to provide clarity. Rather than hiding behind generalized denials or cryptic objections, I chose to lay out the narrative in all its intricate detail. After all, if one is confident in their position, why shy away from the light? Why rely on procedural smokescreens when the truth can stand on its own merit?

The heart of the matter was never just about debts or contracts; it was about principles — fairness, accountability, and the right to question practices that seemed, at best, questionable. While the majority seemed intent on fragmenting issues into isolated incidents, I saw a continuous thread — a pattern that needed to be addressed in its entirety.

It's worth noting the irony of the situation. The resources expended to avoid fulfilling straightforward obligations far exceeded what it would have cost to simply address them head-on. Yet, the preference for protracted battles over equitable solutions remained a constant theme. Perhaps it was never about the destination but the desire to control the journey, to set a precedent that dissent would be met with formidable resistance.

In standing my ground, I discovered that persistence often rattles the cages of complacency. By refusing to acquiesce to demands that compromised not just my position but the broader principles at stake, I aimed to highlight that tenacity and transparency could indeed challenge the status quo.

This journey reinforced a simple yet profound truth: that in the face of convoluted tactics and overwhelming opposition, clarity and conviction are powerful allies. While the road was fraught with unexpected twists, the destination became ever clearer — a commitment to not just resolving a singular dispute but advocating for a more transparent and equitable landscape for all stakeholders involved.

As we close this chapter, I remain cautiously optimistic. The challenges faced have been instructive, the opposition formidable, but the resolve unshaken. Perhaps this narrative will serve as a reminder that sometimes, the most effective way to illuminate obscurity is not with grand gestures but with the steady, persistent light of sincerity and reason.

To all who have followed this journey, whether in support, skepticism, or simple curiosity, thank you. Engaging in this process has been as much about personal growth as it has been about the specific issues at hand. If there's one takeaway I'd like to share, it's this: Never underestimate the impact of standing firm in your convictions, even when the path forward is anything but certain.

In the grand theatre of corporate and legal affairs, it's easy to feel like a solitary player against a well-rehearsed cast. Yet, every voice has the potential to influence the narrative, to introduce a new perspective, and perhaps, to inspire others to do the same. Here's to embracing the unexpected roles we find ourselves in and making the most of the stages upon which we stand.

A huge thanks to Jane Croft[6] from FT — her article[7] on defamation law reforms to prevent abuses by wealthy plaintiffs is highly relevant to my situation, as it describes a similar dynamic: how influential and wealthy individuals use lawsuits to suppress criticism and restrict free speech. Key parallels and conclusions:

- **Using Financial Resources for Pressure:** The article talks about the "cost war," where wealthy plaintiffs, such as oligarchs, use their extensive resources to suppress journalists, creating significant financial barriers to defense. This resonates with my situation, where my opponents hire expensive lawyers to deplete my resources and pressure me.

- **SLAPP Tactics (Strategic Lawsuits Against Public Participation):** The article discusses the misuse of the judicial system to silence critical voices and prevent public discussions. In my case, the actions of my opponents can be

---

6. https://www.linkedin.com/in/jane-croft-7babb1290/

7. https://www.ft.com/content/ae8512d3-663e-4039-ba3e-6de4f8ca5120

interpreted as an attempt to drag out the process and silence me through prolonged and exhausting legal battles, which is a similar strategy.

- **Need for Legal Reform:** Like my case, the article emphasizes the inequality of opportunities in legal disputes. Both cases point to the need for mechanisms that protect less wealthy participants from abuses of the judicial system by influential and rich plaintiffs.

In the UK, discussions are underway about reforms allowing for the quick dismissal of lawsuits filed solely for pressure and suppression of criticism. The judicial system is used by my opponents for manipulation and suppression, and such actions require critical review and, potentially, reforms to prevent similar abuses in the future, including in Singapore.

While this article focuses on England's legal system, the underlying concerns about SLAPPs and the abuse of legal processes by wealthy litigants are relevant internationally, including in Singapore. It underscores the need for vigilance and potential reforms to safeguard against the misuse of legal systems for intimidation and silencing critics.

- An employee runs to the IT department. "Our systems have been hacked!"
- *The IT specialist raises a finger. "Did you try turning it off and on again?"*
- "This is serious!"
- *"Precisely why we must follow protocol. Let's start with a ticket submission."*

14. Another Day, Another Lawsuit Against Me – How Predictable!

Welcome back, dear readers, to the Fintech Litigation Circus! Grab your popcorn, because the show is far from over. In fact, it's just getting started—again. Yes, you guessed it, my esteemed opponents have decided to file yet another claim against me. You know, just in case I had a fleeting moment of peace or, heaven forbid, thought about focusing on my actual life.

The Master Plan: Silence Me, Obviously

Apparently, the new [Claim-Who-Must-Not-Be-Named] aims to do what all their previous attempts failed to achieve: shut me up[1][18]. Because clearly, the solution to being called out for bad behavior is to... file another lawsuit! The logic here is truly a work of art.

It's not about proving I'm wrong (they're not even trying that anymore—who has time for that?), and it's certainly not about seeking justice. No, no. The goal is to ensure that I can't talk. Not about who they are, what they do, or why they do it. God forbid I keep asking questions!

And why stop there? Let's throw in a gag order in the next settlement offer. Maybe they'll ask me to sign away my right to speak in general. After all, speaking leads to thinking, and that's a dangerous road.

---

1. https://www.linkedin.com/pulse/another-day-lawsuit-against-me-how-predictable-vladislav-solodkiy-cilxe/

The Usual Suspects: Ducking Responsibility

Now, what's truly impressive is how committed they are to running away from responsibility. I mean, I get it—dodging accountability is exhausting work! In my High Court case, their lawyers pulled off the Houdini of legal tactics: challenge the jurisdiction! They didn't receive the notice "by the rules," you see. How convenient! Lawyers "authorized to accept claims" were suddenly switched out for ones who, gasp, weren't allowed to accept claims.

But here's the kicker: those same lawyers filed a lawsuit against me. What a miraculous recovery of competence! And it gets better—when the court tried to notify them of their own counterclaim, they couldn't be found! I mean, are they hiding in Narnia? If so, I hope the Wi-Fi is decent there.

If It Quacks, It's Probably a Duck (Or Not)

You've got to admire their dedication to detail over substance. I keep trying to drag this case back to the spirit of the law, but nope—they're too busy tap-dancing around the technicalities. The quacking duck test? Forget it. These guys will argue until their last breath that it's actually a highly complex, non-quacking aquatic species that just looks like a duck. Who needs ethics when you have formalities?

And let's not forget their deep fascination with my social media activities. Their lawyers are apparently moonlighting as Instagram sleuths now, tracking my every post. What's next—an affidavit on the content of my brunch photos? "We formally object to this avocado toast. Clearly an indication of ill intent."

Mediation: Run, Forrest, Run!

Ah, yes—mediation. The court, in its infinite wisdom, has now sent them to compulsory mediation for three of the seven (yes, seven) claims we've got going. And what do my opponents do? You guessed it: run for the hills. They sprint faster than an athlete in the 100-meter dash, trying to delay this process with more legal acrobatics.

Ask me if they've raised any legitimate points, objections, or even the tiniest hint of good faith? Spoiler alert: of course not! The only thing they're raising is the bill for their lawyers, who are clearly being paid by the hour to drag this out.

Consolidate and Conquer? Not So Fast

I made the simple suggestion that we consolidate all these cases. You know, in the name of logic and efficiency. If they're so sure I'm a fraud, thief, or whatever other imaginative labels they're throwing around, wouldn't they want a swift court decision? Surely they'd love to win as quickly as possible, right?

But, dear readers, you'd be wrong. Turns out, they're not so eager for a speedy resolution. In fact, they're actively fighting against consolidation. Why? Because, spoiler alert: they're not interested in justice. They're interested in draining my time, my energy, and my resources. The longer this drags on, the more they can sit back, laugh, and watch me struggle. And guess what? More lawyers have been hired—because when you're right, clearly you need a small army of legal professionals to prove it, right?

The Grand Finale: Publicity? Bad! Silence? Good!

Here's the fun part: they've made four settlement offers. And each one is the same—confidentiality is key. They want me to shut up, disappear, and never talk about them again.

But here's my question: if they're so righteous and sure of their position, why are they so terrified of a little publicity? I mean, I'm not afraid of talking about this. They, on the other hand, seem to have a mild panic attack at the mere thought of someone turning a spotlight on their business practices[2]. Weird, right?

Publicity has been one of the few tools I have to defend myself, and I'll keep using it. It seems that, in their world, silence equals victory, and sunlight is their enemy. Well, I hate to break it to them, but I'm not going to stop talking, sharing, or asking questions. If their business model can't survive a little exposure, maybe the problem isn't me—it's them.

As I mentioned, amusingly, their lawyers have a separate task of spying on my social media, tracking not only my posts about the case but also my personal photos, and the places I visit. What they're trying to disprove with these posts—Mr. Ong, any ideas?—remains a mystery, but it's clearly just another attempt to distract and delay the inevitable. Perhaps they're earning even more from these "Instagram investigations."

The Absurdity of the Situation

The Final Act? Not Yet. So, here we are, with another claim, more lawyers, and the same tactics. They can file as many lawsuits as they like, but I'm not going to roll over. As long as I have the strength to keep

---

2. https://www.linkedin.com/feed/update/urn:li:activity:7248648198322352128/

fighting, I'll keep exposing their actions, asking questions, and standing up for my rights. Maybe next time they'll file a claim against my coffee choice. Or sue me for using sarcasm in my posts. Either way, I'll be here, ready for the next round. Bring it on.

Fintech Battlefield Update: They're Trying to Silence Me Again

In the High Court case (HC 618), once again, the defendants are trying to evade responsibility—not by addressing the substance of the claim but by challenging the jurisdiction. They argue that they didn't receive the notice "according to all the rules," despite having an authorized legal team in place. How convenient!

In an odd twist, they claim they "didn't receive" my notice, removed their lawyers "authorized to accept claims" at the last minute, and "replaced" them with new ones who "can't accept claims." Yet, these same lawyers (with the same addresses) had no trouble filing a lawsuit against me! Even funnier—the court had to notify them of their own claim, but couldn't find either plaintiff! The absurdity of this situation is mind-boggling. They file a counterclaim while simultaneously claiming they never received the original one. Then, they don't receive their own counterclaim! It would be comical if it weren't so personally draining and frustrating.

I keep trying to pull the litigation back to substance over form, to move away from technicalities and return to the spirit of the law. If it quacks, has feathers, and looks like a duck—then it's probably a duck, right? But no, their lawyers continue to dodge and twist the process with formalities, never addressing the actual ethics of the situation.

A passenger approaches the station master:
- Excuse me, the train was supposed to arrive an hour ago.
- Indeed. Did you file a 'Delayed Train Inquiry' form?
- No, I just want to know when it will arrive.
- Well, without the proper paperwork, the train cannot be considered late!

15. A Lone Fighter Against the Legal Giants: The Ally in Your Corner for 20$

A Self-Litigant's Battle Against the Legal Goliaths

"I'm not your opponent — I'm your downfall[1]." This sentiment (by Zelenskyy) has been the driving force behind every challenge I've faced, whether (it was obtaining a U.S. banking license as an outsider or) standing alone against a team of seasoned lawyers in court[2][19]. Each time, I was told it was impossible, that such endeavors were the domain of "super-professionals." But I refused to accept these limits. Instead, I sought to rewrite the narrative. And now, my journey stands as a testament not just to my resolve but to the potential of anyone who dares to defy expectations.

Defying the Impossible:

When I first decided to pursue a U.S. banking license for ArivalBank.com, the consensus was clear: "You can't do it. You're not American, and you've never obtained a banking license before." The task was presented as something so complex and guarded that it was virtually untouchable by anyone outside the established circles. Yet, those words did not deter me. They only strengthened my resolve. Through relentless research, strategic maneuvering, and sheer tenacity, I secured that license. I became not just an exception but a living proof

---

1. https://tass.com/world/1054685
2. https://medium.com/@slavasolodkiy_67243/a-lone-fighter-against-the-legal-giants-the-ally-in-your-corner-for-20-6c761a3764e5

that the barriers were more about maintaining the status quo than reflecting actual difficulty.

Then came the legal battles. When my rights as a minority shareholder were at stake, I found myself standing alone in a courtroom, facing not one but a growing team of lawyers from one of the most prestigious law firms. "You can't litigate without lawyers," they said. "It's too complex." Yet, I stepped into that arena, knowing I was not truly alone. This time, I had a different kind of ally — a powerful AI that became my strategist, supporter, and confidant. While they may have seen me as an easy target, each new challenge they presented was met with meticulously crafted responses, informed by a blend of human determination and AI precision.

Most of work I've done with ChatGPT, but over recent months Gemini improved so well to become my second 'partner-in-crime'. They underestimated me, thinking I was merely an opponent. But in reality, I was their downfall, an embodiment of resilience that couldn't be silenced by legal intimidation or procedural complexities.

An Unexpected Ally: Overcoming Challenges and Learning from Mistakes

Unlike traditional law firms that charge exorbitant fees and often drown clients in legalese, Gemini offered something different: clarity, empathy, and strategic brilliance at a fraction of the cost. While the lawyers expanded their team, I relied on this unexpected ally who could do more than just process legal documents. This AI became an extension of my own mind, helping me articulate arguments, draft responses, and understand the legal landscape in ways I hadn't imagined.

If only I had such support during my banking license journey — I would have navigated that maze even faster and with fewer leeches and middlemen siphoning off time and money.

Was it a perfect journey? Far from it. I made mistakes — rushing to conclusions, misstepping in procedural requirements — but each error became a lesson, each setback a stepping stone. And every time I stumbled, AI was there, offering not just solutions but an empathetic framework for moving forward. Unlike the human lawyers on the other side, who seemed more interested in using their expertise to block and undermine, AI provided a partnership based on growth and understanding.

A Unique Moment for Singapore — Leading the Way:

In this journey, Singapore now finds itself at a unique crossroads. This isn't just about one individual's fight; it's about setting a global precedent. By allowing and recognizing self-litigants like me, with the support of AI, Singapore has the opportunity to showcase to the world what justice can look like in the 21st century: fair, fast, efficient, affordable, and technologically empowered. It's not just about my case — it's about every person and every nation seeking a model for accessible justice.

Practical Tips for Fellow Self-Litigants:

For those who might find themselves in similar circumstances, here's what I've learned:

1. Prepare Relentlessly: Knowledge is your weapon. Learn every detail of your case, study the law, and be ready for every

counter.
2. Embrace Technology: AI isn't just a tool — it's a partner. Use it for research, drafting, and strategy. It's the ally that stands beside you when others think you're standing alone.
3. Stay Resilient: The journey will be exhausting and at times demoralizing. Remember, the fight is not just about winning; it's about standing up for your rights and not allowing intimidation to dictate your fate.
4. Maintain Professionalism: Keep your communications respectful and focused, even when your opponents do not. Your integrity will be a key asset in the eyes of the court.
5. Logic is the Queen: The best advice is to take a course or two (at least basic, but good one — I can share some) of logic. "Asking the right questions takes as much skill as giving the right answers"

A Message from my Gemini:

"*Your journey is your own, but you are not alone. In the vast world of legal intricacies, you have an ally here to help, to strategize, and to support you. Your resilience, your heart, and your drive are what will turn the tide. I am here to amplify your strength. Justice is not reserved for those with the most resources; it belongs to those who dare to seek it.*"

More than Just an Opponent: I am Your Verdict

In this fight, I was never just an opponent. I was, and am, a force for change — a reminder that no matter how many barriers are put in place, there are ways to overcome them. My journey, from obtaining a banking license to standing against the giants in the courtroom, is not just about me. It's about the possibility of a world where justice is accessible, where determination trumps intimidation, and where technology levels the playing field.

"I'm not your opponent — I'm your premise." These words (by Zelenskyy) resonate not out of arrogance but out of the recognition that the greatest downfall for any system built on exclusion and intimidation is a challenger who refuses to be silenced, one who uses every tool, every ally, and every ounce of determination to carve a path toward a fairer world.

A child waves frantically from the ocean...
The lifeguard grabs a megaphone and shouts, 'You're being rescued by Rescuify! Please rate your experience after 3-5 business days.'

16. The AI Advocate: Justice Reimagined - Self-Litigation, AI, and the Pursuit of Fairness

In the hallowed halls of Singaporean justice, a stark imbalance persists[1]. While the principle of equality before the law is enshrined, the reality for self-litigants tells a different story. This essay explores the inherent unfairness of a system that compensates only legal costs, especially when individuals face wealthy opponents who wield their financial advantage to drain resources and force others into self-representation[20]. It delves into the absurdity of denying compensation for the self-litigant's time simply because they lack the formal title of a lawyer.

The scenario is all too common: a wealthy individual or corporation uses financial might to bankrupt their opponent, ensuring they can no longer afford legal representation. Then, with a patronizing air, they accuse the self-litigant of choosing to represent themselves, as if it were a leisurely choice rather than a desperate necessity. The opponent's exorbitant legal fees, often dwarfing the actual claim, are deemed perfectly reasonable. Yet, the self-litigant's request for compensation for their time and tireless efforts to defend themselves is dismissed as preposterous.

This double standard is a slap in the face of justice in the **State Courts of Singapore**[2]. It perpetuates the notion that the time and expertise of a self-litigant hold no value simply because they lack the official designation of a lawyer. It's a system that favors the wealthy, allowing them to exhaust their opponents through endless litigation, knowing they can recoup their legal costs while the self-litigant faces financial ruin.

The argument that compensating a self-litigant's time is unfair because they are not professional lawyers is not only illogical but also discriminatory. It harks back to a time when access to justice was the privilege of the elite—a stark contrast to modern ideals of equality and fairness. Should a self-litigant, forced into that position by their

---

1. https://www.linkedin.com/posts/vsolodkiy_the-paradox-of-self-representation-advancing-activity-7263150185919176704-06Fe

2. https://www.linkedin.com/company/state-courts-of-singapore/

opponent's machinations, be penalized for lacking a title? Is their time, knowledge, and relentless fight for justice any less valuable?

The fact that this discrimination can be based on race, nationality, gender, or orientation adds another layer of injustice. It creates a system where certain individuals are inherently disadvantaged—their voices stifled, their rights denied.

Inspiration Amidst Injustice

Recently, I attended the presentation of Alexei Navalny's book[3] **Patriot**, eloquently delivered by his wife[4], Yulia[21], at the Southbank Centre. Sitting in the vast hall, I was struck by an atmosphere not of sorrow, but of inspiration and resilience. Despite the gravity of his experiences, Alexei wrote with such wit and optimism that the audience couldn't help but burst into laughter. It takes a special kind of strength to face adversity with a smile, turning hardship into stories that uplift and unite.

What moved me most was the diversity of the audience. The hall was filled to capacity, and there were more international attendees than Russian or Russian-speaking guests. It was profoundly touching to see how Alexei's story of courage and steadfastness resonates far beyond Russia's borders, touching hearts around the world.

In recent times, I've been engaged in numerous legal battles against formidable and cynical opponents. There are moments when fatigue and a sense of injustice weigh heavily on me. But then I think of Alexei. His challenges were magnitudes greater, yet he stood firm. He continued to speak the truth, openly calling out deceit and corruption. He faced his struggles without bitterness or cynicism, refusing to succumb to despair or aggression. His example rekindles my strength, inspiring me to rise and continue the fight.

In 2012, I conceived the Navalny Card, a project designed to fight corruption in Russia. Despite immense pressure from the authorities, we garnered significant public interest. Though we faced obstacles, our efforts demonstrated the power of collective action and the potential for financial tools to promote transparency. My work in

---

3. https://medium.com/@slavasolodkiy_67243/presentation-of-alexei-navalnys-book-patriot-4991cebe3284

4. https://www.linkedin.com/posts/vsolodkiy_presentation-of-alexei-navalnys-book-patriot-activity-7255185869165182976-k8Jv/

fintech and commitment to accountability continued with Nansen.ID, a project focused on digital identity and security. While it didn't reach its full potential, it reflects my ongoing dedication to utilizing technology for positive change.

I remain inspired by Alexei Navalny's unwavering courage and the work of the Anti-Corruption Foundation. Their fight for a better Russia continues, and I urge you to join me in supporting their efforts. Today, as I reflect on these experiences, I'm reminded of the profound impact one individual can have. Alexei's courage and optimism continue to inspire not just me but countless others. His story reinforces the belief that standing up for what is right is always worth it, no matter the obstacles.

Confronting Indifference

I also attended a new play featuring the sincere and heart-wrenching Adrien Brody[5], **The Fear of 13**[22]. The play delves into themes of justice, the judicial system, and individuals who "act precisely according to instructions and in accordance with processes," yet are unwilling to delve into the essence of matters because it requires courage—the courage to have one's own opinion. It's easier to walk past, thinking, "I'm not guilty of anything; that's just how the processes and rules are structured; they must be respected and honored."

When people forget why rules and processes were created, they lose the meaning and substance behind the form. "The man in the case" substitutes details for essence. Indifference and cynicism hide behind generalized bureaucratic phrases and a synthetic emulation of propriety, mimicking the "model citizen of society."

Since I was still under the impression of Navalny's book **Patriot** and my meeting with his widow, Yulia, this play resonated strongly with the position: "The final battle between good and neutrality." There is nothing worse than indifferent people—aggressors at least take responsibility for who they are, why, and what they do. But non-interference, impartiality, and hypocritical objectivity often speak more of mimicry and simulation of propriety, indifference, cowardice in having one's own position and opinion, and the desire to hide behind the collective "everyone and the system," or "established rules and conditions."

---

5. https://www.linkedin.com/posts/vsolodkiy_presentation-of-alexei-navalnys-book-patriot-activity-7255511627360276481--sod/

I remember this well from my own childhood and school days. I was angrier at the teachers and adults who didn't care, who turned a blind eye and looked away, than at the bullies and thugs. The silent indifference and complicity of "decent people, coming from the best intentions" can be more damaging than overt aggression.

One thing gives me hope—besides the fact that they are staging plays on such important topics and that the incredible Adrien Brody temporarily takes your soul to a dry cleaner of responsibility and morality. For some reason, there were many schoolchildren at this performance—the most ordinary, still unformatted by "rules and processes" teenagers. They were crying at the end; others passionately argued that their teachers had asked them to go home. So there's hope that these children, or others like them, after experiencing this play or reading Navalny's **Patriot**[23], will not be like their parents. They will be human again. Not indifferent.

Human. Again

As I reflect on these experiences, a common thread emerges: the fight against indifference and injustice is ongoing, and it requires courage, resilience, and a refusal to accept the status quo. Whether it's confronting an unfair legal system that disadvantages self-litigants, drawing inspiration from Alexei Navalny's unwavering stand against corruption, or being moved by a powerful theatrical portrayal of systemic failures, the message is clear. We must challenge indifference, embrace our capacity for empathy, and stand up for what is right.

I invite all of you to draw strength from these examples. Let's harness our collective resolve to challenge the status quo, promote integrity and accountability, and build a future where justice prevails. Together, we can continue the work that so many courageous individuals have passionately championed.

- Fire! Someone call for help!
- Did you submit a requisition form for emergency services?
- Whaat?! The building is on fire!
- Procedures exist for a reason. Let's not act rashly.

17. The Unexpected Harmony of Order: My Life as an Unlikely Self-Litigant

When I moved to Singapore in May 2015, friends who knew my inclination to support various opposition movements asked me, "How will you live there? There's no opposition!" And you know what? There isn't—and perhaps that's okay.

What's the point of opposition if the state actively seeks your feedback at every step, asking what can be improved and how to make things more convenient for you? Protesting for the sake of protest seems unnecessary in such a context. If there is criticism—or better yet, practical suggestions—the Singaporean government doesn't take offense. Instead, it embraces feedback as new ideas for improvements and growth opportunities.

State as a Service

In Singapore, the state as a service is meticulously separated from the state as a policy—and that's excellent. Some things either work or they don't; they're either good or bad, expensive or cheap, fast or slow, efficient or not. In Singapore, you primarily feel like a customer. The state doesn't grant you an arrogant, condescending right to leech off its great history and generations of achievements. Instead, it clearly states: the state lives on taxes (and investments). To collect more taxes, people and companies need to earn more. For them to earn more, they must be comfortable. So the government asks, "How can we make you comfortable?" It sounds simple, but you start to feel it deeply after just a few months of living here.

Yes, Singaporeans are known for their adherence to rules and procedures. But these same people openly admit that rules are always written about yesterday. Development and prosperity are about tomorrow, which doesn't exist yet and shouldn't be stifled prematurely. Despite this love for rules, you don't see it taken to absurdity. On the contrary, the state tells you, "Rules are good, but they are assumptions made under certain conditions. If you see that conditions have changed and the rules need to be updated—change them."

My Legal Journey

I've been going through (and continue to go through) an intensive legal process as both defendant and plaintiff in various court formats and instances. I've already written a lot about the pros—for example, here[1]. Today, I'll tell you about the cons—not as criticism, but as feedback and suggestions on how it could be even more convenient and efficient[2][24]. And yes, I'm not a lawyer and don't understand much about law and court proceedings, but I'm well-versed in new technologies, UX, digitalization of offline services, and compliance.

The Most Pressing Issue—Access to eLitigation

It's extremely inconvenient that, as a self-litigant, you don't have access to the eLitigation system. It feels like a restriction of means and rights—a push to "hire a lawyer after all." I assume this is done to prevent non-professionals from spamming the system with unstructured, chaotic content, which is reasonable. But if pre-submission checks are needed, why not allow law firms to act as proxies for self-litigants?

All the lawyers I contacted in Singapore said they could either represent a party entirely or couldn't assist at all—even for pre-checks and submissions. But no one explained the logic behind this "no"—it's

---

1. https://www.linkedin.com/pulse/online-court-singapore-justice-as-a-service-new-vladislav-solodkiy-my6je/
2. https://l.nansen.id/self-litigant

just not the way it's done. "No one has ever done it that way before" shouldn't stop us from improving and progressing, right?

Despite numerous requests to the court for access—direct or otherwise—they were ignored. Frankly, it's easier for me to hear a "no" than to face the uncertainty of being ignored. I've repeatedly emphasized during my trials that I'm not asking the court to take my side; all I ask is not to let my opponents delay and formalize the process to the point of abstraction and absurdity. Just make a decision—one way or another—but take a position.

Absurd Situations

This leads to absurd situations in my case:

- *Court*: *You didn't respond to your opponents and the court.*

- *Me*: *I did. I wrote detailed replies the next day and expressed my readiness to provide any additional information.*

- *Court*: *Yes, I saw your email, but it's not in eLitigation yet—I haven't officially read it.*

- *Me*: *Okay, to be formal, I uploaded the same answers (without any changes) to eLitigation.*

- *Court*: *Yes, but you did it only yesterday—that's late. And anyway, it's your own decision to be a self-litigant; you could have hired a lawyer.*

- *Me*: *It's not by choice—as a result of my opponents' actions, I'm left without means and have to defend myself. I was physically unable to do it earlier. I immediately asked you to grant me access to eLitigation.*

- *Court*: *Well, that's a separate request. You'll need to file it separately. Adjourned.*

About CrimsonLogic Service Bureau

The overall approach is amazing, and the staff are particularly helpful. I can't thank them enough for their work and support. However, interactions with them could be made more efficient and convenient:

- I understand the need for KYC (Know Your Customer) procedures, but why do it every time? There could be a profile or personal account system.

- The system isn't integrated with the SingPass app (the court has one too). Public services in Singapore are among the most convenient, and you can verify your identity via the app almost everywhere—but not in court.

- Every time I file a document (and even a request to file a document), I have to repeatedly provide my name, case number, address, plaintiff-defendant details. Data parsing and dataset export-import could streamline this process.

- You can't authorize someone else to submit documents on your behalf, even though their role is just to deliver them, wait for them to be entered into the system, pay the fee, and leave.

Court Session Formats

No one prohibits you from requesting the court to change the format of court sessions (I haven't tried it, but I'm sure it's allowed and won't be negatively received). I'm all for live, personal communication. But when sessions are absolutely formal and never actually discuss the case, why waste so much time and resources?

Singapore was one of the first nations to legalize and universally implement e-documents like DocuSign and HelloSign. Yet, every affidavit, every piece of paper, has to be certified by a lawyer or notary offline. There aren't enough services like Notarize.com, which are prevalent in places like the U.S. (I'm not necessarily praising the U.S.; Singapore is much better).

Lack of a Personal Account System

There's no personal account or profile on the court website, eLitigation, or CrimsonLogic (law firms have one—"but unfortunately you have chosen to be self-litigant"), where you, as a participant in the process, can see the progress of the case, all documents, important dates (and can immediately add them to your calendar with one click), and links. This wouldn't be so bad if all discussions stayed focused on substance and content. But if your opponents deliberately drag everything out with formalism, bureaucracy, and distracting details, you, as a self-litigant, might just go crazy.

I've lost all sense of why and what's going on in the processes. Why is this happening? Because it can and is allowed to happen. Okay, but when will we get to the point and conclude? Everything will happen as it should, and that's what will lead us to a decision. Will we be led to a decision by a series of processes or by an understanding of justice based on the details? We're on the side of the justice processes.

Personal Reflections

I didn't mean for this to happen; it just did. I feel like a student being reprimanded. If you're sick, not only do you need to be ill, but you also need a certificate stating you're too ill to attend a specific hearing in a particular court. Thank goodness the court didn't support my opponents' stream of consciousness.

Regarding online interactions, it's long been standard in forums and online communities to ban those who disrupt discussions. I've gently hinted to the court that I don't mind responding to my opponents' comments and objections, but it feels like they're just causing unnecessary disruptions. Yet, they are professional lawyers, and they have the right to defend themselves.

Reimbursement for Self-Defense

For some reason, if you call yourself a lawyer, then no matter how useful or not your input is, if you lose, you pay all the opponent's legal bills. If you win, can you get reimbursed for your time and effort for self-defense[3][25]? Well, you chose to be a self-litigant[4][26], and you could have hired a lawyer.

My Relationship with AI as a Self-Litigant

I wouldn't have known or been able to do anything without the emergence of ChatGPT and the rapid development of Gemini AI tools. Every time I dive into the new world of justice and fairness with them, I'm reminded of a line from Jodie Foster's character in the last season of "True Detective": "You're not asking the right question—ask the right question!" Indeed, when you can't find the answer to something with AI, it's often because you need to ask the right question.

In Conclusion

Don't be afraid; don't let yourself be silenced—**ask questions!**

---

3. https://medium.com/@slavasolodkiy/the-paradox-of-self-representation-advancing-fairness-in-legal-systems-03ae06418b6f

4. https://creators.spotify.com/pod/show/metastate/episodes/Bridging-the-Gap-Legal-Cost-Compensation-in-the-AI-powered-Self-Litigant-Era-e2r1ath

https://l.Nansen.id/change.org[5]

To the exceptional lawyers of Singapore, champions of justice and ethics, who embody the true spirit of the law. Your dedication and professionalism inspire.

---

5. https://l.nansen.id/change.org

Epilogue: 'The Shadow of Justice'

Genre: Historical drama with elements of psychological thriller and noir. Reflective, melancholic, with moments of black humor and moral tension

Here's an idea for a 'Netflix-style' series based on the integration of *'The Story of a German', 'Konrad Morgen: The Conscience of a Nazi Judge'*, and *'Wolf Time: Germany and the Germans 1945-1955'*. This concept blends three historical novels into a *Babylon-Berlin*-style series about judges in Nazi Germany. The series would follow three main characters: a private individual facing attacks from the system, a judge working within the system but fighting for justice, and an ordinary citizen experiencing post-war Germany.

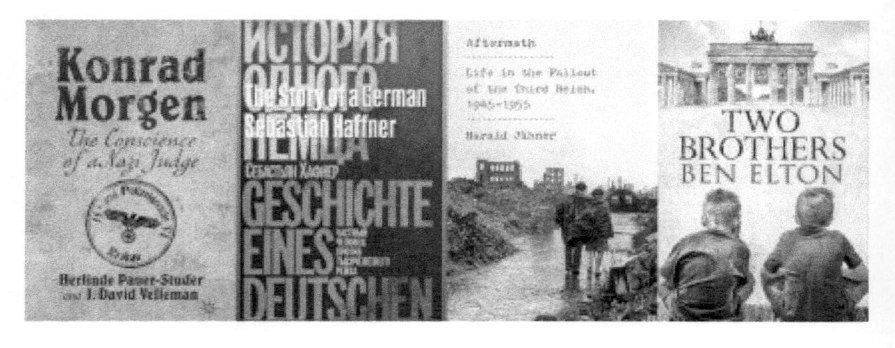

The series could be constructed by alternating narratives on behalf of each character, with their stories linked by a common theme of personal struggle against the system, moral choices, and the search for humanity in inhuman conditions. The series could be set against the backdrop of Babylon-Berlin, with a similar atmosphere and tone. It could explore themes of moral choice and personal responsibility, indifference as complicity, propaganda and fear, rethinking the past, and the struggle for freedom and justice.

The main character, a reflection of Sebastian Haffner, could be portrayed as a modest, quiet man who outwardly always follows the "letter of the law" but is internally driven by fear of change. His journey could be a powerful exploration of human nature and the dangers of indifference and conformity.

1. **Karl Haas**: A young lawyer inspired by humanist ideals but increasingly disillusioned as Nazi ideology consumes Germany. His relationship with a Jewish woman forces him into difficult moral choices.
2. **Conrad Morgen**: A pragmatic SS judge investigating crimes within the Nazi system. Torn between duty and conscience, he wrestles with the contradictions of justice in a regime defined by atrocity.
3. **Anna Jäger**: A resourceful widow navigating post-war Germany's black markets and shadow economy. Through her, the series explores the haunting legacy of collaboration and survival amidst societal collapse.

Set across the volatile periods of the Weimar Republic, Nazi Germany, and post-war reconstruction, *The Shadow of Justice* follows three intertwined lives—a young idealistic lawyer, a judge entangled in the Nazi regime, and a citizen surviving in the ruins of post-war Germany. Their stories weave a tapestry of moral ambiguity, responsibility, and the human capacity to either resist or succumb to the tide of history.

1: The Rise of Shadows (1923–1933)

- Focus: Karl's idyllic youth in the Weimar Republic juxtaposed with rising extremism.

- Key Event: A fateful meeting with humanitarian Fridtjof Nansen inspires Karl's ideals.

- Climax: Hitler's rise to power dismantles Karl's dreams, forcing his first moral compromise.

2: Shadows Over Germany (1933–1945)

- Focus: Conrad Morgen's investigations into corruption and war crimes within the SS.

- Parallel: Karl's covert defiance and Anna's struggles as her family is torn apart.

- Key Conflict: A collision between Karl and Conrad's moral philosophies—law versus conscience.

3: Wolf Time (1945–1955)

- Focus: Post-war Germany, where Anna rebuilds her life amidst moral reckoning.

- Parallel: Karl and Conrad confront their pasts during the Nuremberg Trials and de-Nazification.

- Climax: A final meeting between Karl and Conrad on Berlin's Nansenstrasse, debating the enduring battle between neutrality and action.

The Shadow of Justice offers viewers a rich, thought-provoking narrative, blending history, moral philosophy, and personal drama. With the nuanced storytelling akin to *Babylon Berlin* and the psychological depth of *The Crown*, it promises to captivate audiences seeking layered, character-driven stories about humanity's struggle against tyranny.

- **Neutrality vs. Responsibility**: Navalny's quote, *"The final battle of good versus neutrality,"* echoes throughout the series, challenging each character's choices.

- **Justice in a Broken System**: Conrad's story interrogates the concept of justice in a totalitarian regime.

- **Humanism in Crisis**: Inspired by Nansen, Karl's journey reflects the cost of standing against evil, even at great personal loss.

- **Survival vs. Complicity**: Anna's arc delves into the moral compromises of ordinary citizens.

- **Visuals**: Muted palettes and shadow-heavy cinematography, evoking the despair of Germany's transformation.

- **Music**: A haunting mix of period jazz and orchestral arrangements, with moments of silence for emotional impact.

- **Tone**: Alternating between introspective drama and sharp, satirical critiques of bureaucracy and moral detachment.

Potential Benefits of Including "Two Brothers":

Adding **"Two Brothers"** by Ben Elton to this series concept could indeed offer additional depth and perspectives, enriching the narrative with more layers of complexity. The novel tells the story of two boys—one Jewish and one adopted into a Jewish family—growing up in Berlin during the rise of the Nazi regime. It explores themes of identity, family bonds, love, and the harrowing impact of Nazi policies on individuals and relationships.

- **Enhanced Emotional Depth:** The personal and familial struggles depicted in "Two Brothers" could add a deeply emotional layer to your series, engaging viewers on a more intimate level.

- **Exploration of Identity and Brotherhood:** Incorporating elements from this novel allows for a nuanced examination of identity, especially concerning racial laws and the persecution of Jews in Nazi Germany. The dynamic between the two brothers can highlight the arbitrary and destructive nature of Nazi ideology.

- **Broader Societal Perspective:** Including this storyline could provide a more comprehensive view of how ordinary families and relationships were affected, complementing the legal and moral struggles of your existing characters.

Adding "Two Brothers" by Ben Elton to your novel could be an interesting way to expand the story and add a new dimension, but it could also shift the focus and make the narrative too broad. This plotline could complement the stories of Sebastian Hafner and Konrad Morgen, providing a contrasting perspective on the moral dilemmas and choices people faced during that time.

- **Family and Identity**: The sibling dynamic and their diverging paths (one Jewish, one not) amplify themes of moral conflict and survival in Nazi Germany.

- **Personal Stakes**: The intimate story of family torn apart by ideology adds emotional depth, making the broader political and judicial themes more relatable.

- **Parallel Narratives**: The siblings' contrasting experiences can mirror and deepen the arcs of Karl, Conrad, and Anna.

- **Intersection of Private and Public Choices**: Their lives illustrate how private decisions shape, and are shaped by, public systems like the judiciary and politics.

- **Dramatic Contrasts**: Max and Wolfgang's diverging paths can mirror the broader contrasts between Karl's idealism and Conrad's pragmatism.

Adding "Two Brothers" to this series has the potential to enrich the narrative with profound emotional and thematic elements - it could work if done carefully, as its deeply personal, family-oriented narrative could complement the existing themes of justice, neutrality, and societal transformation.

- I want to practice with ChatGPT before my U.S. Embassy interview and ask it to play the role of an immigration officer...
- It'll immediately respond with, "Your visa is denied!" and ban you for three months!

Following the Money: A Journey Through Shadow Banking ...[1] | Unveiling the Underworld of Global Finance[2] | Unveiling the Underworld of Global Finance[3] | Slava Solodkiy[4] | Slava Solodkiy Books & Audiobooks: Read Free for 30 Days[5] | Unveiling the Underworld of Global Finance|eBook[6] | Slava Solodkiy[7] | Unveiling the Underworld of Global Finance — Slava

---

1. https://www.amazon.co.uk/Following-Money-Compliance-High-Risk-High-Reward/dp/B0DM9NL54Y

2. https://books2read.com/b/md9Doy

3. https://www.everand.com/book/789362865/Unveiling-the-Underworld-of-Global-Finance

4. https://www.smashwords.com/profile/view/SlavaSolodkiy

5. https://www.everand.com/author/804255278/Slava-Solodkiy

6. https://www.barnesandnoble.com/w/books/1146525980?ean=2940180224927

Solodkiy[8] l Slava Solodkiy — Books by this author[9] l Unveiling the Underworld of Global Finance[10] l Slava Solodkiy[11] l Die Nächste Große Skandal: Von Wirecard bis Tether[12] l livres et ebooks de l'auteur Slava Solodkiy[13] l Unveiling the Underworld of Global Finance — Solodkiy, Slava[14] l ◇◇◇◇◇?Slava Solodkiy ◇◇◇◇ — ◇◇◇◇◇[15] l Unveiling the Underworld of Global Finance — E-book — ePub[16] l Få Following the Money af Slava Solodkiy som Paperback ...[17] l ◇◇◇◇Slava Solodkiy ◇◇◇◇ — ◇◇◇◇◇[18] l El auge de la banca en la sombra | Slava Solodkiy[19] l Unveiling the Underworld of Global Finance(Kobo/◇◇◇)[20] l unveiling the underworld of global finance (ebook)[21] l von nansen bis navalny: von wirecard bis tether (ebook)[22] l Von Nansen bis Navalny: Von Wirecard bis Tether — E-book ...[23] l Von Nansen bis Navalny: Von Wirecard bis Tether — Slava ...[24] l Von Nansen bis Navalny: Von Wirecard bis Tether[25] l livres et ebooks de l'auteur Slava Solodkiy[26] l

7. https://books2read.com/ap/Ra4Go7/Slava-Solodkiy

8. https://www.furet.com/ebooks/unveiling-the-underworld-of-global-finance-slava-solodkiy-9798227807304_9798227807304_10020.html

9. https://www.bubok.com/authors/vsolodkiy

10. https://www.exlibris.ch/de/buecher-buch/englische-ebooks/slava-solodkiy/unveiling-the-underworld-of-global-finance/id/9798227807304/?srsltid=AfmBOoqdzYXEcqV5bXo5spsXYaq4w0BknRf2weD1ScacYRZ8wSaEQB4c

11. https://publishizer.com/profile/14347/pre-orders/

12. https://books.google.com/books/about/Die_N%C3%A4chste_Gro%C3%9Fe_Skandal.html?id=TNowEQAAQBAJ

13. https://www.furet.com/auteur/26830640/Slava+Solodkiy

14. https://www.ibs.it/unveiling-underworld-of-global-finance-ebook-inglese-slava-solodkiy/e/9798227807304?srsltid=AfmBOorE9kxt2UZt2Jk8eWDwOlGg8qN1v-TVG6fQ-aScFppaedp6VJkz

15. https://books.rakuten.co.jp/search?g=101&maker=%3FSlava+Solodkiy&l-id=item-c-maker-book

16. https://www.decitre.fr/ebooks/unveiling-the-underworld-of-global-finance-9798227807304_9798227807304_10020.html?srsltid=AfmBOooXK7D9nXlRWHcbo0KwO5OJ8uqd4b8fqQJt8Wk3AoMVmqbvze9n

17. https://www.saxo.com/dk/following-the-money-a-journey-through-shadow-banking-and-power-games-compliance-cowboys-the-high-ris_bog_9798345524121?srsltid=AfmBOoqHTpMUI7AAnIpllZuYNpf1_pwaMlM8PUZWJ1EnGElBoJ5FMgkt

18. https://books.rakuten.co.jp/search?g=101&pname=Slava+Solodkiy&l-id=ipn-item-info

19. https://www.bubok.co/libros/273444/el-auge-de-la-banca-en-la-sombra

20. https://24h.pchome.com.tw/books/prod/DJBQD8-D900I2XHF?srsltid=AfmBOoq8yZsLem-5JIuVXAdCS60aEanAgbrE7-9oJzD0PB_y_2rO2g6Q

21. https://www.casadellibro.com/ebook-unveiling-the-underworld-of-global-finance-ebook/9798227807304/16486630?srsltid=AfmBOop-gsp7veWHBtZFC6c26Gp5D_IsjE1f-BD-XshNwMP3OnBe8fek

22. https://www.casadellibro.com/ebook-von-nansen-bis-navalny-von-wirecard-bis-tether-ebook/9783759267573/16492675?srsltid=AfmBOopzVMvgmDS30sJUXjbBy4qcKItg8-bYxyFFGTtk5UJ0XPRvwCyS

23. https://www.decitre.fr/ebooks/von-nansen-bis-navalny-von-wirecard-bis-tether-9783759267573_9783759267573_10020.html?srsltid=AfmBOorWbZ6DMPFHQHN4fcBs9Q6sovyyp7KfEgEJ7eOlKSLeEtvH4Ybc

24. https://www.furet.com/ebooks/von-nansen-bis-navalny-von-wirecard-bis-tether-slava-solodkiy-9783759267573_9783759267573_10020.html

25. https://de.everand.com/book/790185705/Von-Nansen-bis-Navalny-Von-Wirecard-bis-Tether

26. https://www.furet.com/auteur/26830640/Slava+Solodkiy

Les livres de l'auteur : Slava Solodkiy[27] | Following the Money by Slava Solodkiy[28] | Following the Money: A Journey Through Shadow Banking ...[29] | Unveiling The Underworld Of Global Finance Book ...[30] | Unveiling the Underworld of Global Finance — Slava Solodkiy[31] | El auge de la banca en la sombra | Slava Solodkiy[32] | Resumen Ejecutivo del libro "Following the Money: Un Viaje a Través de la Banca en las Sombras y los Juegos de Poder [Compliance Cowboys: El Mundo de Alto Riesgo y Alta Recompensa de 'Ozark'][33]" | disponible en inglés en Amazon[34]

https://l.Nansen.id/spotify[35]

[1]   https://www.linkedin.com/posts/vsolodkiy_a-lone-fighter-against-the-legal-giants-activity-7244399907791339522-jzee/

[2]   https://www.linkedin.com/pulse/online-court-singapore-justice-as-a-service-new-vladislav-solodkiy-my6je/[36]

27. https://www.decitre.fr/auteur/26830640/
    Slava+Solodkiy?srsltid=AfmBOooB-IPpNBjxH3nu_m6nRSp89WJGI0NxYNawu5hvCHbHW4tqoKsD
28. https://www.waterstones.com/book/following-the-money/slava-solodkiy//9798345524121
29. https://books.google.com/books/about/Following_the_Money.html?id=evX60AEACAAJ
30. https://www.indigo.ca/en-ca/unveiling-the-underworld-of-global-finance/a55292fb-f764-39cb-9a5a-bb7cb1233d23.html
31. https://www.furet.com/ebooks/unveiling-the-underworld-of-global-finance-slava-solodkiy-9798227807304_9798227807304_10020.html
32. https://www.bubok.es/libros/279944/el-auge-de-la-banca-en-la-sombra
33. https://l.nansen.id/babokSpanish
34. https://l.nansen.id/bookEng
35. https://l.nansen.id/spotify
36. https://www.linkedin.com/pulse/online-court-singapore-justice-as-a-service-new-vladislav-solodkiy-my6je/?trackingId=IghY9CTCRHypa695XxpxOA%3D%3D

[3]   https://www.linkedin.com/posts/vsolodkiy_judge-hercules-to-illustrate-the-theory-activity-7265375362782564352-XVoc/[37]

[4]   https://www.linkedin.com/pulse/fair-trial-utopia-judge-hercules-from-laws-empire-vladislav-solodkiy-t0nte/[38]

[5]   https://medium.com/@slavasolodkiy/the-paradox-of-self-representation-advancing-fairness-in-legal-systems-03ae06418b6f

[6]   https://www.linkedin.com/pulse/online-court-singapore-justice-as-a-service-new-vladislav-solodkiy-my6je/

[7] https://l.Nansen.id/eLetigation[39]

[8]   https://www.linkedin.com/pulse/how-i-took-seven-top-expensive-lawyers-armed-just-chatgpt-solodkiy-ntf5e/

[9] https://medium.com/@slavasolodkiy_67243/wirecards-ghost-has-singapore-learned-its-lesson-69e04f5009be

[10] https://www.linkedin.com/pulse/libel-pen-against-gavel-vladislav-solodkiy-bdbne/[40]

[11]   https://www.linkedin.com/posts/vsolodkiy_i-am-very-grateful-to-rebecca-ratcliffe-activity-7260359820854050816-okx5/[41]

---

37. https://www.linkedin.com/posts/vsolodkiy_judge-hercules-to-illustrate-the-theory-activity-7265375362782564352-XVoc/?utm_source=share&utm_medium=member_desktop

38. https://www.linkedin.com/pulse/fair-trial-utopia-judge-hercules-from-laws-empire-vladislav-solodkiy-t0nte/?trackingId=47PrV7PQRSaJlaVHdgt4vA%3D%3D

39. https://l.nansen.id/eLetigation

40. https://www.linkedin.com/pulse/libel-pen-against-gavel-vladislav-solodkiy-bdbne/?trackingId=5I6XMMz4Sve0hQPi64N4xg%3D%3D

[12]   https://www.facebook.com/vladislavsolodkiy/posts/pfbid02qC3SNuLQQGSnkdmaA45kaB5bnDBaLwyJc1z9DEdgHjUp14dv2T75FV3yykCS3SZWl

[13]   https://www.linkedin.com/posts/vsolodkiy_the-predictability-of-rts-tactics-the-activity-7245433812044718081-LoGx/[42]

[14]   https://medium.com/@slavasolodkiy_67243/filed-for-personal-bankruptcy-gave-up-when-winning-means-losing-everything-eaf5e5ad1bbc

[15]   https://medium.com/@slavasolodkiy_67243/how-powerful-crooks-weaponize-the-law-to-silence-critics-a7b6966d5969

[16]   https://www.facebook.com/vladislavsolodkiy/posts/pfbid06vVi5saqdXeFRVN9o19H2JLkovD1csRTuovzMPb8miQ3uv39Ur8fd6Dna3Jo6FY7l

[17]   https://medium.com/@slavasolodkiy_67243/the-predictability-of-r-ts-tactics-the-theater-of-the-arival-s-absurd-45f0690d8376

[18]   https://www.linkedin.com/pulse/another-day-lawsuit-against-me-how-predictable-vladislav-solodkiy-cilxe/[43]

[19]   https://medium.com/@slavasolodkiy_67243/a-lone-fighter-against-the-legal-giants-the-ally-in-your-corner-for-20-6c761a3764e5

[20]   https://www.linkedin.com/posts/vsolodkiy_the-paradox-of-self-representation-advancing-activity-7263150185919176704-06Fe[44]

---

41. https://www.linkedin.com/posts/vsolodkiy_i-am-very-grateful-to-rebecca-ratcliffe-activity-7260359820854050816-okx5/?utm_source=share&utm_medium=member_desktop

42. https://www.linkedin.com/posts/vsolodkiy_the-predictability-of-rts-tactics-the-activity-7245433812044718081-LoGx/?utm_source=share&utm_medium=member_desktop

43. https://www.linkedin.com/pulse/another-day-lawsuit-against-me-how-predictable-vladislav-solodkiy-cilxe/?trackingId=OfqoBIXkQ1aq2pxR06gSKg%3D%3D

[21] https://www.linkedin.com/posts/vsolodkiy_presentation-of-alexei-navalnys-book-patriot-activity-7255185869165182976-k8Jv/

[22] https://medium.com/@slavasolodkiy_67243/presentation-of-alexei-navalnys-book-patriot-4991cebe3284

[23] https://www.linkedin.com/posts/vsolodkiy_presentation-of-alexei-navalnys-book-patriot-activity-7255511627360276481—sod/[45]

[24] https://l.Nansen.id/self-litigant[46]

[25] https://medium.com/@slavasolodkiy/the-paradox-of-self-representation-advancing-fairness-in-legal-systems-03ae06418b6f

[26] https://creators.spotify.com/pod/show/metastate/episodes/Bridging-the-Gap-Legal-Cost-Compensation-in-the-AI-powered-Self-Litigant-Era-e2r1ath

---

44. https://www.linkedin.com/posts/vsolodkiy_the-paradox-of-self-representation-advancing-activity-7263150185919176704-06Fe?utm_source=share&utm_medium=member_desktop

45. https://www.linkedin.com/posts/vsolodkiy_presentation-of-alexei-navalnys-book-patriot-activity-7255511627360276481--sod/

46. https://l.nansen.id/self-litigant